3.95

Büchner

Woyzeck

Edward McInnes

Professor of German
University of Hull

University of Glasgow French and German Publications
1991

University of Glasgow French and German Publications

Series Editors: Mark G. Ward (German)
Geoff Woollen (French)

Consultant Editors : Colin Smethurst
Kenneth Varty

Modern Languages Building, University of Glasgow,
Glasgow G12 8QL, Scotland.

First published 1991
Reprinted 1994

Printed by Castle Cary Press, Yeovil, Somerset BA20 2HP

ISBN   0 85261 341 5

CONTENTS

For my Brother James

A Glaswegian and Lover of German Literature

PREFACE

All references to *Woyzeck* in the body of the text are to Georg Büchner, *Sämtliche Werke und Briefe*, ed. W.R. Lehmann, Vol.1 (Hamburg, 1967). This edition is in my view still the most authoritative and the only one generally accepted by Büchner scholars. However, I am aware that aspects of this edition are controversial and gladly acknowledge the valuable contributions of critics like Richards, Poschmann and Guthrie (listed in the bibliography) to the continuing debate on the form of the text.

I would like to thank Mark Ward for giving me the opportunity to write at some length on this powerful and intensely challenging play and for his very generous editorial help. I also feel indebted to Mrs Catherine Ready for preparing the manuscript with her usual efficiency and good humour and to my daughter Alison who helped me understand aspects of Woyzeck's illness I had not grasped before.

Edward McInnes
University of Hull
September 1991

****

'Wenn das Buch, das wir lesen, uns nicht
mit einem Faustschlag auf den Schädel
weckt, wozu lesen wir
das Buch?'

Kafka

CHAPTER ONE

BÜCHNER AND THE GERMAN DRAMATIC TRADITION

Woyzeck, as every literary historian accepts, is a work of intense, startling originality. It is a play which anticipates the most fundamental developments in the drama for almost a century but which has no recognisable predecessor or model. *Woyzeck* seems in fact to have come into being in direct opposition to the controlling traditions of the German drama and in open rebellion against the practice and ethos of the contemporary theatre.[1] By comparison with *Woyzeck* the work of the most radical 'progressive' dramatists of Büchner's day, the so-called Young Germans, seems very restricted in aspiration and all but devoid of creative energy.[2] Even in the context of the dramatist's own work *Woyzeck* represents a development which still seems unforeseeable and from most points of view utterly astonishing. All in all, it is not going too far to say that this is a play which is quite incongruous, both in conception and technique, with any earlier or contemporary work and which, as far as I can see, owes nothing to existing theories of the drama.

Equally surprising is the fact that Büchner, as far as we know, did not engage in any lengthy, coherent planning before he set about writing *Woyzeck*, or attempt to work out in a systematic way just what he was seeking to achieve. The only indications we have that Büchner was edging his way towards this his most novel, ambitious dramatic work were oblique and essentially allusive. These are to be found not in a theoretical discussion or abstract statement of intent but in a work of fiction, his novella *Lenz*, in which he sought to re-create imaginatively the spiritual collapse of the anguished young dramatist of the *Sturm und Drang*, Jakob Michael Reinhold Lenz. Through this intense intuitive identification with the disaffected playwright of the 1770's (who was in Büchner's time almost completely forgotten) he attempted to confront the nature of his own revolt against the main traditions of the German drama and to probe the artistic possibilities inherent in his own changing and as yet unfocussed aims as a playwright.

In his novella Büchner presents Lenz as the supreme iconoclast of the German-speaking drama who, alone and single-handed, challenged the

inflexible authority of classicist poetics and freed the genre to reach out
to quite new, provocative modes of realism - a freedom which in
Büchner's view the literary establishment in Germany was still seeking
to suppress in the 1830's. The young playwright of the *Sturm und
Drang* , as Büchner sees him here, is a visionary genius of a
disconcertingly down-to-earth and abrasive kind who pursued the one
deceptively simple end of making the drama the sensitive organ of
immediate social awareness. Büchner's Lenz is a playwright gripped by
the driving conviction that the drama could only regain its power as a
dynamic cultural force if it could embrace directly the experience of the
ordinary, unremarkable people who constituted the overwhelming bulk
of the population. Only a drama which could grasp the profound, often
repressed and barely recognised, tensions which rent the experience of
his contemporaries as they struggled to come to terms with their
existence in an increasingly alien, depersonalised society could bring the
theatre again into the heart of the real world where people actually
struggled and suffered and make it again (as, for instance, in
Shakespeare's time) a potent, shaping vehicle of lived experience. All
of this, however, as Büchner was well aware, brought Lenz into direct
and open conflict with the basic aesthetic and moral assumptions
governing the literary world in the late 18th century.

In the so-called *Kunstgespräch* in the middle of the novella Büchner's
Lenz vehemently attacks the idealistic tendencies of contemporary
German art and literature and attempts to describe his own aims and
achievements as a practising playwright:

> Ich verlange in allem Leben, Möglichkeit des Daseins, und dann ist's gut;
> wir haben dann nicht zu fragen, ob es schön, ob es häßlich ist, das Gefühl,
> daß was geschaffen sei, Leben habe, stehe über diesen beiden, und sei das
> einzige Kriterium in Kunstsachen. Übrigens begegne es uns nur selten, in
> Shakespeare finden wir es und in den Volksliedern tönt es einem ganz, in
> Göthe manchmal entgegen. Alles übrige kann man ins Feuer werfen. Die
> Leute können auch keinen Hundsstall zeichnen. Da wolle man idealistische
> Gestalten, aber alles, was ich davon gesehen, sind Holzpuppen. Dieser
> Idealismus ist die schmählichste Verachtung der menschlichen Natur. Man
> versuch es einmal und senke sich in das Leben des Geringsten und gebe es
> wieder, in den Zuckungen, den Andeutungen, dem ganzen feinen, kaum
> bemerkten Mienenspiel; er hätte dergleichen versucht im 'Hofmeister' und
> den 'Soldaten'. Es sind die prosaischsten Menschen unter der Sonne; aber
> die Gefühlsader ist in fast allen Menschen gleich, nur ist die Hülle mehr
> oder weniger dicht, durch die sie brechen muß. Man muß nur Aug und
> Ohren dafür haben ... Der Dichter und Bildende ist mir der liebste, der mir
> die Natur am wirklichsten gibt, so daß ich über seinem Gebild fühle, alles
> übrige stört mich (*Werke* 1, pp.86f.)

Büchner is presenting Lenz here as a searching social realist who brings the drama in a quite abrupt, uncompromising way into the everyday reality of the home and the market-place. In so doing Lenz (as Büchner sees it) sweeps aside the disabling conventional distinctions between the poetic and the mundane, the momentous and the banal, and lays bare the supreme self-deceiving lie which lurks at the heart of all idealistic conceptions of art.[3] His main achievement as a playwright, as Büchner's Lenz himself regards it, is that he penetrated behind the conventional façades of life in contemporary society and probed the experience of ordinary individuals from within. He saw their existence not - Lenz claims - as their social superiors saw it, but in their own terms and, as it were, through their own eyes.

In his novella Büchner sees this new kind of drama created by Lenz as supremely innovative and liberating. In this new realistic mode the playwright dispenses with action in the traditional sense of an unfolding conflict between powerful individuals who pursue their vast, historically significant ends. Lenz's drama is essentially inward-looking and exploratory. Its impelling energies stem not from external collision but from the working out of deeply-lying, largely wordless pressures in the consciousness of the characters themselves - pressures which they often struggle in vain to understand and negotiate.

This drive to internalise the dynamic of the drama, manifests in Büchner's view a quite momentous change of perception. Lenz's conception of an inward psychological form, as it is defined here in the novella, rests on two basic assumptions which are both fundamentally incompatible with classicist dramatic theory. The realistic inner drama which Büchner's Lenz is advocating here, presupposes that the psychic existence of the lowly, non-heroic individual is in itself morally and imaginatively significant. He assumes that in this hidden, inner world of even the 'most prosaic people under the sun' there lie tensions substantial and powerful enough to sustain the dramatic structure, to replace, that is, conventional and outmoded forms of plot and intrigue.

This is bound up with an even more basic and powerful conviction which Büchner's Lenz openly asserts but does not explore. He insists namely that it is the individual's emotional experience which ultimately makes him what he is. The individual, he claims, is most profoundly himself, most authentically human, in his deepest feelings of love, fear and yearning, feelings which spring inescapably from his seminal experience as a human being and which he therefore shares with all men everywhere. Lenz is here assuming that as an emotional being the individual transcends the conditioning pressures of society and culture which differentiate and divide people, often bitterly, in their communal existence. When they are gripped by intense emotion all men - Lenz declares - partake of a fundamental life, common to all, which underlies all arbitrary historically determined barriers and which is the sustaining foundation of human identity.

This sense of humane revealing purpose informs Lenz's conception of his new drama and lends it its wider ethical significance. His questioning realistic mode, committed to the diagnostic methods of observation and analysis, is shaped at its deepest core by a vision of an underlying communality of human experience, a vision of the ultimate kinship of all human kind.

Critics over the years have repeatedly failed in my view to emphasize the extent to which Büchner in this *Kunstgespräch* is reading his own compelling but unformed artistic preoccupations into the work of the 18th century playwright.[4] In fact, some of the main artistic impulses he attributes here to Lenz seem to me to bear very little relation to the latter's actual plays. It is noticeable, for instance, that Büchner almost completely disregards the strong comic energies in Lenz's dramatic conception. There is a clear discrepancy between the inward, psychological realism Büchner's Lenz proclaims here, and the formal structure of *Der Hofmeister* or *Die Soldaten* which depends heavily upon the playwright's use of the conventional mechanisms of traditional comic plotting.

This is symptomatic. Büchner is so concerned to elevate the qualities of sympathetic insight and pathos as the shaping impulses of Lenz's work that he is forced to ignore the constantly mocking sardonic thrust of his imagination. In emphasizing Lenz's will to affirm the essential human significance of his humble figures Büchner disregards this deeply satiric, deflating tendency of Lenz's perception. The view of his work Büchner is keen to assert here does not allow him to grasp the peculiarly ambiguous, unsettling character of Lenz's vision and thus to do justice to the innovative, equivocal tragi-comic mode which the young dramatist sought to realise in the 1770's. Büchner in fact, it seems to me, is strangely insensitive to what we now tend to see as the distinctive force of Lenz's divided, quizzical way of seeing - his attempt to present the dramatic action at once as touching and absurd, and in so doing to hold irony and pathos in vibrant, dislocating tension.

This all strongly suggests that in his preoccupation with playwright of the *Sturm und Drang* Büchner was intuitively reaching forward, feeling his way ahead. In his reading of Lenz's plays he was trying in some profound imaginative depth of himself to clarify his own emergent perceptions of a new kind of contemporary realistic tragedy. It is as if the force of this inner quest drove him instinctively to embrace those impulses in Lenz's comic mode which could foster his own creative aspirations, draw them more fully into his conscious artistic awareness. There were, Büchner seems to have sensed, tendencies in Lenz's vision and dramatic method which he, Büchner, had to develop and bring to fruition in the late 1830's in ways responsive to the increasingly empirical, sceptical outlook of the late 1830's.

When we look at Büchner's interest in Lenz from this point of view, we can see, I think, that it was driven in large part by a need to engage his sense of his own progression as a dramatist. It served at once to focus his growing sense of distance from his earlier dramatic work and to clarify the practical means by which he could pursue his quest for a new, more radical mode of dramatic realism. His preoccupation with the work of the 18th century playwright thus seems to have sharpened his critical awareness of his aims and his technical insight, while at the same time providing him with vital creative stimulus. When he came to write *Woyzeck*, however, Büchner was completely on his own. He knew he was breaking new ground and that in entering such new territory he was defying more than ever before the expectations of his contemporaries. But even Büchner himself can scarcely have sensed how enduringly influential his play was going to be.

NOTES

1. See M. Benn, *The Drama of Revolt*, Cambridge, 1979 pp.255ff.. W. Hinderer, *Büchner. Kommentar zum dichterischen Werk*, München 1977, pp.65ff.
2. E. McInnes, *Das deutsche Drama des 19. Jahrhunderts*, Berlin, 1983, pp.17ff.
3. I. Stephan and H.-G. Winter, 'Ein vorübergehendes Meteor?' *J.M.R. Lenz und seine Rezeption in Deutschland*, Stuttgart, 1984, pp.64ff.
4. R.C. Cowen, *Das deutsche Drama im 19. Jahrhundert*, Stuttgart 1988, pp.82ff.. R. Hauser, *Georg Büchner*, New York, 1974, pp.54ff.. is one of the few critics who have emphasized the anachronistic character of some of the ideas which Büchner attributes to the 18th century playwright. See also Benn, *The Drama of Revolt*, pp.88f..

CHAPTER TWO

THE GENESIS OF THE PLAY: THE WOYZECK CASE AND THE CLARUS REPORTS

Büchner seems to have told his friends very little about the writing of *Woyzeck*. In his letters from the summer and autumn of 1836 - at least in those that have survived - his references to his work in progress are very guarded and often appear slyly inexplicit. This has created considerable problems for Büchner scholars, and it is only recently that they have come by means of tortuous processes of deduction and elimination to a broad general agreement about when he actually wrote the play. Most critics now seem to accept that he began *Woyzeck* in the late spring of 1836, worked on it intermittently in the summer and autumn of this year and that he was still struggling in vain to complete it when he was taken terminally ill at the beginning of February of 1837.[1] But beyond this very little is known for sure.

It is ironic that the writing of *Woyzeck* should have been such a private, hidden affair since the play itself in its impelling preoccupations is 'public' in such an open and radically provocative sense. To Büchner's contemporaries it would have been at once apparent that *Woyzeck* was not a product of the dramatist's subjective imagination, that it was not a 'fictional' play but one based on an actual, well known murder-case. We can see just how revolutionary Büchner's intentions were in this respect. No German dramatist before him had ever attempted to achieve this kind of directly topical, documentary significance. He had, it is true, based his first play *Dantons Tod* (1835) on detailed historical records, but in *Woyzeck* Büchner was dealing with a subject which was much more recent and closer to home, and which was, above all, still the focus of intense controversy among his contemporaries. This is the crucial point. In *Woyzeck* the playwright was not just out to re-enact the story of the unemployed, ex-soldier from Leipzig who had murdered his mistress and had subsequently been tried and executed for his crime. He was driven rather to confront this deeply disturbing case by a need to intervene in a vital, on-going public debate, a debate which Büchner clearly believed would be of vital significance for the future of German society. In dramatising the story of *Woyzeck* he was deliberately seeking to extend and intensify a controversy which in his view many of his contemporaries, were attempting, consciously or unconsciously to ignore.

This is not to deny that Büchner had a close and committed interest in the figure of Johann Woyzeck, in his life and experience as a unique individual. But he was concerned to see this murder in the context of a group of similar murder-cases which had also given rise to uneasy and protracted public discussion. When he studied the records of the trial and conviction of Woyzeck he was looking for basic underlying links between this and other equally squalid and perplexing murders, most notably those committed by Daniel Schmolling in Berlin in 1817 and by Johann Dieß in Darmstadt in 1830.[2] Büchner's study of these murders obviously impinged deeply on his attempts to penetrate the complexities of the Woyzeck case and probably shaped his understanding of it more profoundly than he realised. And indeed the similarities are very striking. Schmolling and Dieß were, like Woyzeck, poor, displaced individuals from the lower depths of society who (again like him) had killed their mistresses. Most significant of all, however, was the fact that all three had shown clear symptoms of mental abnormality before they had perpetrated their crimes.[3] It was this above all that had brought these cases into the forefront of public attention and made them the subject of extended comment in legal and medical journals. They all in their different ways raised the same crucial and deeply disturbing issue of the murderer's responsibility for his crime. The question which tormented some of Büchner's contemporaries was whether these strangely withdrawn and seemingly psychotic individuals were morally accountable for their actions and had been justly subjected to the full severity of the law.

These cases thus opened up fundamental and far-reaching ethical questions in the most direct and unsettling way. They seemed to many enquiring, progressive people in the 1830's to pose a serious challenge to the established system of justice, not just the mechanisms through which it operated but to the whole structure of moral and social assumptions on which it was based. Underlying such uneasy scepticism about the processes of the law in contemporary society one can see in retrospect deeper-lying, officially suppressed doubts about accepted notions of personal freedom and responsibility and the scope of man's powers as an autonomous moral agent.

But despite the fact that Büchner seems to have become more and more aware of the representative, focussing importance of the Woyzeck case and he made considerable efforts to come to terms with the actual murder which had taken place on the 21st of June 1821 in Leipzig. He went to great lengths to find out all he could about Woyzeck's life, crime and subsequent trial, and about the intense controversies which continued to surround the case more than fifteen years later. In this sense Winkler was quite right to insist more than sixty five years ago that Büchner regarded Woyzeck's crime and trial as a 'piece of history', a series of particular, minutely recorded events which he had to investigate as a pragmatic historian.[4] From this point of view Büchner's approach to the subject-matter of his play appears as a consequential development of that which he adopted when he set out to dramatise the climactic events in the life of Danton in the previous year.[5]

There was certainly no shortage of detailed evidence about Woyzeck's killing of Frau Woost. This was by far the best known and fully debated murder-case in Germany in the 1830's. At his disposal Büchner had not only the official documents of the complex and extremely protracted trial with its many judgments, appeals and conflicting submissions, and the very extensive newspaper coverage of the whole notorious case. He also had one other very productive source which in the end was to prove of determining importance. In view of the intensely controversial nature of the trial the court in Leipzig had requested two reports on the mental condition of Woyzeck from the medical officer of the city, Hofrat Dr. Johann Clarus. The first of these was submitted in September 1821 and served to prepare the way for the death-sentence which was eventually passed by the court. This sentence provoked serious doubts in many quarters, however, and after the execution of Woyzeck had been postponed twice, the court, finally yielding to incessant pressure, commissioned Clarus in October 1822 to prepare a second, more detailed assessment of psychological state of Woyzeck at the time of the murder.[6]

These reports, and especially the second much more extensive one which was published in book form in 1824, were of vital significance to Büchner. It is clear that they provided him with new and more differentiated information about the character and outlook of Woyzeck than he had been able to obtain elsewhere. But these reports also seem to have given the dramatist a sharp, precipitating insight into the minds of those who had sat in judgment over Woyzeck and despite all the intractable doubts of many serious minded laymen condemned him to death. The study of Clarus' reports acted on Büchner's creative imagination as an abrasive force of provocation. It drove him, it seems, to confront tensions in his perception of the case and to seize his artistic intentions with a new incisive clarity.

There is no doubt that Clarus approached the task imposed on him by the court with high solemnity and painstaking care. At the same time it is apparent that he seeks to assess the medical aspects of the case not just as a doctor but also as a man very conscious of his eminent civic position and of his consequent responsibility to uphold the framework of moral and legal values which sustained the whole order of society. In his attempt to assess Woyzeck's psychological state he proceeds from the clear, explicit conviction that the individual is free and is therefore responsible for his actions. He repeatedly proclaims the fundamental significance of this conviction. It is not just one article of faith among others, he claims, but the crucial presupposition shaping our understanding of justice and indeed of moral experience in all its forms (*Werke*, 1, pp.488ff.). For Clarus, in other words, the belief in the freedom of man's will is the bedrock of all civilised life; all human institutions - religious, social and legal - and the authority they embody ultimatley depend upon it. His determination to protect the notion of man's moral autonomy drives Clarus to insist that only the most severe mental derangement, a derangement which undermines the very fabric of the individual's selfhood, could be seen as suspending his accountability for his actions (pp.518ff.; 528f.).

The crucial question governing Clarus' deliberations in both his assessments is simple and apparently quite unequivocal. Was it possible for Woyzeck - he asks himself constantly - not to have killed his mistress? Could he have held his murderous rage in check? Only overwhelming proof that Woyzeck's normal mental functions had broken down at the time of the murder, that he was in a state of utter psychic confusion, could be sufficient in Clarus' view to exonerate him from the responsibility for such a terrible crime. Only under these circumstances could be seen as the victim of forces beyond his moral control.

Evaluating all the evidence at his disposal from this pont of view Clarus comes to the clear unhesitating conclusion that Woyzeck was not insane when he committed the murder, and that he was therefore ethically and legally responsible for what he had done.

One of the most striking aspects of these reports by Clarus is the tenacious consistency of his argument. His second submission for all its greater detail and wider scope, just serves to confirm the findings of the first. Although he again interviewed Woyzeck extensively and reassessed the evidence presented to the court before drawing up his second report, Clarus uses his new evidence solely to enforce his initial judgment and to justify the principles underlying his first attempt to assess the murderer's psychic condition. It becomes increasingly obvious in fact that he is really intent on defending himself against those who continued to express their misgivings about his first document. This uneasy defensiveness is particularly evident in the way he consistently tries in his second submission to play down the signs of Woyzeck's inner disorder by attributing them to purely physical causes. He sees Woyzeck's visions, eg., as stemming from problems of circulation, and his symptoms of paranoia as the consequence of his morbid temperament (pp.523ff.). In this way he seeks to 'normalise' the image of the psychological condition of the murderer by showing that he was not swept along by a wild, irresistible dementia, was not the victim of a madness which rendered him insensitive to all normal human compunctions. On the contrary, what made Woyzeck unable to control the violence in his own nature was not in Clarus' view insanity but the gradual weakening of his moral will, a process for which he was responsible. His final surrender to his murderous passion stemmed (Clarus insists) from the undermining of his strength of character by the pressures of a depraved existence spent in drunkenness and sexual dissipation. Woyzeck, in the Doctor's view, was the victim not of mental derangement but of his own freely chosen way of life which had increasingly eroded his moral powers of self-control. For Clarus there is an important moral warning in the fall of Woyzeck which he was keen to impart to young people still in the process of shaping their lives:

> Möge die heranwachsende Jugend bei dem Anblicke des blutenden Verbrechers, oder bei dem Gedanken an ihn, sich tief die Warhheit einprägen, daß Arbeitsscheu, Spiel, Trunkenheit, ungesetzmäßige Befriedigung der Geschlechtslust und schlechte Gesellschaft, ungeahnet und allmählich zu Verbrechen und zum Blutgerüste führen können (*Werke* 1, p.490).

We have no direct record of Büchner's reaction to Clarus' reports. However, the viciously satirical portrayal of the Doctor in his play gives us, I think, a very clear indication of the intense outrage he experienced. We can also see that the attitude of detached, authoritarian aloofness which governs Clarus' attempt to grasp the mental state of Woyzeck was in direct conflict with Büchner's insistence in *Lenz* that only sensitive, sympathetic concern can enable one human being to enter the hidden reality of another's life and touch his deepest wordless anguish and yearning. (See above pp.4f.) In these submissions the dramatist would have looked in vain for any concern on the part of the judging doctor to reach out in compassionate fellow feeling to the hopeless murderer before him. On the contrary, Clarus seems to presuppose throughout that it is precisely his remoteness from Woyzeck, his superiority of intellect and moral awareness, which enabled him to penetrate the impulses determining the behaviour of the murderer. His power to understand and judge - Clarus presumes - stems not from an intuitive sympathy with the mind of the criminal, but from his ability to stand, as it were, outside it and see its corruptness from the standpoint of his own moral assurance. His rôle, as he saw it, was to expose the full insidious depths of Woyzeck's failure and to condemn it, not to sympathise with him and thus to alleviate the burden of his guilt. We can safely surmise, I think, that in Clarus' self-righteous, complacent withdrawal from Woyzeck the dramatist must have seen an example of that 'verachtenden Egoismus' which he describes in a letter in February 1834 as a blasphemous disregard of essential humanity of another being in his need (*Werke* 2, p.423).

If we accept that the dramatist's confrontation with the Clarus reports had a powerful, releasing impact on his creative imagination, we can see at once the extent to which the conception of *Woyzeck* was shaped by Büchner's drive to bring together preoccupations, insights and imaginative perspectives which were disparate and seemingly at odds. It is clear that he was deeply moved by the anguish of the driven, haunted man who became a murderer. This urge to identify himself imaginatively with the figure of the criminal, to assert his profound violated humanity, is one of the most powerful, shaping impulses of Büchner's play and critics from the first have acknowledged both its originality and far-reaching prophetic significance.

This will to close sympathetic involvement with the hero was inseparably bound up, however, with a radical socially critical impetus which in its sheer intensity and searching disaffection goes far beyond anything in the drama of its time. His will to affirm the human dignity of Woyzeck brought with it a concern to lay bare those forces of injustice and oppression which pervaded the life of this deeply divided but complacent society, a society which had, it seems, systematically subjected and demeaned the lowly soldier and now condemned him with the utmost self-righteous severity.

Büchner seems, on the one hand, to be intent on developing a tragic conception which asserts the human standing and significance of the socially disregarded hero and puts him forward as a potent agent of tragic experience, a being able to live out in himself the ultimate yearning and dereliction of tragic suffering.   At the same time, however, Büchner also seems to be working towards a new kind of dissenting, critical tragedy in which the hero appears as the disabled victim of an overwhelmingly hostile world which seems to deny him all rights of existence.

NOTES

1.   See Benn, *The Drama of Revolt*, pp.218ff.
2.   L. Bornscheuer, *Georg Büchner. Woyzeck. Erläuterungen und Dokumente*, Stuttgart, 1976, pp.49-67, reprints some of the important documents relevant to these murder-cases.See also W. Hinderer, *Büchner. Kommentar zum dichterischen Werk*, pp.172ff.
3.   Krause, *Woyzeck. Texte und Dokumente*, Frankfurt am Main, 1969, pp.162f. notes that the three different cases have the following features in common: 'die Zugehörigkeit der Personen zu den unteren und ärmeren Schichten des Volkes, ihre Armut und Bedürftigkeit; jeder der drei Mörder ist Soldat gewesen; sie haben eine Geliebte, mit der sie in engem Verkehr stehen, aber nicht verheiratet sind; die Bedeutung eines unehelichen Kindes; im Fall Schmolling wird es erwartet; im Fall Woyzeck ist nur von einem Kind die Rede, das mit einer früheren Geliebten, also nicht mit der Ermordeten, gezeugt wurde; im Fall Dieß ist das Kind etwa viereinhalb Jahre alt; die Ermordung der Geliebten mit einem Messer (nur im Fall Woyzeck spielt Untreue dabei eine Rolle); herbeieilende Leute nach dem Mord, Festnahme des Mörders, Gerichtsverhandlungen'.
4.   H. Winkler, *Georg Büchners 'Woyzeck'*, (Diss. Greifswald, 1925), p.124.
5.   Büchner himself writes in a letter to his family in July 1835: 'Der dramatische Dichter ist in meinen Augen nichts, als ein Geschichtsschreiber, steht aber über Letzterem dadurch, daß er die Geschichte zum zweiten Mal erschafft und uns gleich unmittelbar, statt eine trockene Geschichte zu geben, in das Leben einer Zeit hinein versetzt ...' (*Werke* 2, p.443).
6.   Clarus' two reports are reprinted in full in Lehmann's edition of Büchner's works, Vol.1, pp.487-549.

CHAPTER THREE

ANALYSIS OF THE DRAMATIC ACTION

I EXPOSITION AND CRISIS

(1) The opening Scene

In Büchner's day, as throughout most of the 19th century, the exposition was generally regarded as a basic, functional part of the dramatic form, but a part which was essentially preliminary to and outside the action proper.[1] Playwrights and literary theorists in Germany in the 1830's accepted that the opening scenes of a play served to reveal the situation of the characters to the spectator or reader thus enabling him to understand readily the events about to unfold on stage. The aim of the exposition was, in other words, to ease the audience into the world of the play as quickly and effortlessly as possible, even if this meant that the dramatic figures often had to tell one another things that they already knew, and that the expository process was usually static, discursive and quite empty of dramatic life.

The opening scene of Büchner's play as we now know it[2] turns all such conventional practice upside down (Sc.1, *Freies Feld. Die Stadt in der Ferne*, p.409). It is intensely, hauntingly dramatic, it positively vibrates with hidden menace, but it denies us the imaginative support and direction which come from a firm grasp of the prevailing situation. At the end of the scene we are assailed by all kinds of unfocussed apprehensions and doubts but we know very little more than we did at the beginning. On stage we see two men gathering sticks in a wood which is evidently not far from a town (p.409). But whereas we would expect a readily intelligible, informative conversation to develop between the two men, Woyzeck and Andres, they remain cut off from one another and never really communicate. While Woyzeck is trapped throughout in horrifying hallucinations which transfix his inner self, Andres, perplexed and increasingly terrified, tries to close his mind to what his friend is saying. In fact, for much of the scene he sings so that he can drown out the sound of Woyzeck's voice. And certainly what Woyzeck is struggling to grasp is quite terrifying. He appears at first to be paralyzed by a vision of a man being beheaded. It then becomes clear that he senses in this the work of the freemasons who, he knows in himself, seek to kill him too. Finally, Woyzeck seems overwhelmed by signs of an appalling divine retribution which threatens to engulf the whole landscape.

There is next to nothing in this scene that we could call expository in any recognised sense. The dramatist gives us very little firm information about the situation which exists and seems in fact intent on denying us the basic facts necessary to understand and respond to the events on stage. We are conscious of being plunged abruptly into a serious crisis, but a crisis which neither of the two dramatic figures seems able to comprehend much less communicate, and which thus remains beyond our reach throughout. Büchner appears in fact to present Andres ironically as a hapless caricature of the traditional figure of the *raisonneur*. Far from drawing Woyzeck into meaningful (and for us informative) discussion he recoils in fearful, bewildered dread from his friend's terrifying visions. And Woyzeck for his part seems so wholly consumed by his nightmare innner certainties that he can only suggest their overwhelming power over him but give no intelligible account of their character or implications.

This opening scene does not draw us into a recognisable world which has a clear and thus reassuring affinity with our own. Throughout the scene the normal contours of everyday reality are eclipsed by the paranoiac horror of Woyzeck's visions which in their dark menace disconcert us profoundly and drive us to anxious questioning and speculation. At the end of the scene we still have no clear idea of the identity of Woyzeck. Only in the last couple of lines are we able to infer that he and Andres are soldiers. But the crucial question which besets us constantly is not who Woyzeck is but how he has come to be in this deranged, psychotic state. What pressures in his experience (we are forced to ask) have so disturbed the balance of his mind and exposed him to such rending delusions of persecution?

The first scene of *Woyzeck* thus draws us into the action of the play not by means of a progressive revelation of definable tensions between the characters but by facing us directly and alarmingly with the blind inner torment of the hero. It confronts us with a process of mental disorder whose origins lie in the unknown past of Woyzeck and whose outcome, we sense, must be calamitous unless some radical, transforming power of healing can bring renewal to his stricken mind.

What is most striking about this opening scene is the uncompromising concern of the dramatist to assimilate expository concern, the revelation of existing circumstances, to an awareness of dramatic development, of uncoiling tension. This is characteristic of Büchner's technique throughout the play. He seems driven as if by instinct to absorb analysis into action and to pursue far-reaching processes of social exposition through the enactment of erupting crisis. This tendency is very evident in the scenes which follow. As Büchner explores the sources of Woyzeck's psychic disorder in the torment of his day-to-day existence, he shows the growing infatuation of Marie, Woyzeck's common-law wife and mother of his child, with the handsome, ruthless Drum Major. He switches attention constantly back and forth between the two centres of concern, the deepening subjection of Woyzeck in society and the irrevocable withdrawal from him of Marie. As we witness her reckless pursuit of her passion we are forced to recognise the unrelenting suffering of Woyzeck at the hands of an alien, destructive world.

(2) The Poverty and social Oppression of Woyzeck

I have been suggesting that the opening scene of *Woyzeck* drives us imaginatively beyond the lonely figure before us and forces us to query the nature of his life-history and experience. Büchner presents the mental crisis of his hero in a way which forces us to ask the most basic far-reaching question: what has happened to this man, what anguish has he suffered which could reduce him to this victimised, psychotic state? The dramatist pursues this implied link between Woyzeck's inner break-down and his everyday life in society in a series of scenes which explore his relations with the middle-class figures who control his existence. These scenes have a much more overtly expository character than the opening one and pursue a radical, abrasively critical purpose. Yet it is worth noting again the force of Büchner's concern to gather up these scenes into the quickening momentum of the tragic development. They are informed, on the one hand, by a powerful sense of the sharpening pressures on the stricken hero; they are also, as I have suggested, closely bound up with the enactment of Marie's infatuation with the handsome stranger who intrudes without warning into her existence.

In these socially exploratory scenes (Sc.5, *Der Hauptmann. Woyzeck* pp.414f.; Sc.8, *Beim Doctor*, pp.417f.; Sc.18, *Der Hof des Doctors* pp.425f.) as in the opening scene of the play, Woyzeck is working. What is most significant, however, is that he is not carrying out his duties as a common soldier which were at this time in themselves notoriously arduous and exhausting. He is doing additional tasks that he

undertakes in order to supplement his income on which he is clearly
unable to live. Indeed in these scenes, as in other parts of the play, he
appears as a man haunted by a dread of poverty, a dread so intense that
he seems to spend almost every waking moment struggling to make ends
meet. If he is not cutting wood, he is shaving his Captain or hiring
himself out to the Doctor as a guinea-pig for his idiosyncratic
experiments.

Büchner draws us to see in these images of what is quite literally
forced labour the symptom of a life pervaded by a terror of complete
destitution.   Constant, unremitting anxiety about money is the
inescapable condition of Woyzeck's day-to-day existence. Whatever the
details of his life as a soldier, whatever the nature of his communal
experience, he is always at a profound emotional level (the dramatist
suggests) a man driven by a chronic fear of not being able to provide
for himself, for Marie and their child.

In the first of these diagnostic scenes (Sc.5, pp.414f.) Woyzeck is
engaged in shaving his Captain. The latter is his commanding officer
and it is evident that he automatically assumes the right to extend his
authority over all areas of Woyzeck's life - social, moral and emotional.
He traps his deferential subordinate (acting here as a hired servant) in a
logical contradiction in order to pronounce him scornfully 'abscheulich
dumm' (p.417). He goes on to condemn Woyzeck as immoral because
he has a child without benefit of clergy. Here, as throughout the whole
encounter the Captain is enhancing his own sense of self-esteem by
asserting his superiority over his unresisting subordinate. In declaring
Woyzeck stupid the Captain vaunts his own intelligence, in denigrating
him as immoral he applauds his own virtue. Many critics have regarded
the Captain as a buffoon, a man foolish rather than evil, and denied that
there is real malice in his attitude to Woyzeck.[3] This ignores in my
view, however, the range and seriousness of Büchner's socially critical
purpose in this scene.

The dramatist's intention becomes fully apparent, I think, in the
central part of the encounter between the two men. Here Woyzeck,
rejected by the Captain as dissolute, insists that he too, poor and
uneducated as he is, has a deep yearning for goodness. He simply could
not afford the marriage which would have made his child legitimate, he
explains. He and people like him are bound by a terrible necessity:

> Wir arme Leut. Sehn Sie, Herr Hauptmann, Geld, Geld. Wer kein Geld
> hat. Da setz eimal einer seinsgleichen auf die Moral in die Welt. Man hat
> auch sein Fleisch und Blut. Unseins ist doch einmal unseelig in der und der

andern Welt, ich glaub' wenn wir in Himmel kämen so müßten wir donnern helfen. (p.415)

Ignoring the Captain's condescending attempts to soothe him Woyzeck continues:

> Sehn Sie, wir gemeine Leut, das hat keine Tugend, es kommt einem nur so die Natur, aber wenn ich ein Herr wär und hätt ein Hut und eine Uhr und eine anglaise und könnt vornehm reden, ich wollt schon tugendhaft seyn. Es muß was Schöns seyn um die Tugend, Herr Hauptmann. Aber ich bin ein armer Kerl. (p.415)

Woyzeck is here - though he would be horrified to think it - effectively pricking the complacent self-righteousness of the Captain. For if virtue, as Woyzeck is insisting, is the by-product of a prosperous and privileged way of life, then it follows that someone like the Captain can claim no credit for his moral virtue and have no grounds for condemning the behaviour of the poor and deprived which falls short of his lofty norms.

Büchner shows that the Captain completely fails to grasp the point of Woyzeck's argument here, even though what he says is quite clear and directly relevant to what they are discussing. The dramatist seems to be implying that the Captain's incomprehension stems not so much from simple obtuseness as from some much deeper, inarticulate force of resistance: from the fact that Woyzeck's claim runs counter to the basic assumptions governing his view of himself and the world, and is to him quite literally unthinkable. The radical moral relativism which Woyzeck has been asserting directly contradicts the Captain's unspoken belief that his moral and intellectual superiority is intrinsic to himself as an individual, something inborn and divinely ordained, and thus finally independent of external factors like wealth and social position.

For the dramatist the Captain's failure to understand Woyzeck's argument is therefore not just the result of a bumbling self-importance or harmless vanity but reflects a basic socially conditioned attitude which Büchner terms 'Aristokratismus', the tendency of the 'educated and well-to-do minority' to deny their essential human solidarity with the poorer, less privileged people who constitute the overwhelming bulk of the population (*Werke* 2, p.455).

Here, it seems to me, the dramatist is taking over one of the main socially critical concerns which exercised Lenz in the 1770's and shaped the conception of his two comedies *Der Hofmeister* and *Die Soldaten* which Büchner so greatly admired. Like his predecessor in the *Sturm und Drang* he is exposing the drive of the ascendant social class of his day to see itself, consciously or unconsciously, as a separate, superior group which exists essentially outside the body of society as a whole. The dominant middle-class in the 1830's in Germany - Büchner is suggesting - resists full social involvement and thus genuine corporate responsibility. Its driving interest lies rather in asserting its pre-eminence, and as a result it inevitably sees more lowly social groups as existing solely to serve its needs, to enhance its wealth and power, and to heighten its self-esteem. This, in Büchner's view, engendered in the members of the prepotent bourgeoisie an attitude of disdain towards those less fortunate and powerful and a will to reduce and dehumanize which, as he asserts in his famous letter to his family of February 1834, is the most heinous contempt for the Holy Spirit in all men (*Werke* 2, p.423).

In this scene, *Der Hauptmann. Woyzeck*, the dramatist seeks to lay bare deep-seated social tensions which for all their immense destructive force remain largely unacknowledged in the normal continuum of collective existence. In the scenes which explore Woyzeck's relations with the Doctor, the other powerful representative of the ascendant middle class, he extends this analysis of class-antagonisms in a more openly polemical and strident form. Büchner is concerned to show here (Sc. 8, pp.417f.; Sc.18, pp.425f.) that the Doctor, like the Captain, is impelled by a remorseless, unexpressed drive to assert his authority over Woyzeck. As an eminent medical researcher and Professor of rank he assumes the right to treat the soldier as one of his laboratory animals whose *raison d'être* lies solely in his usefulness to his experiments. Whatever his express convictions the Doctor gives himself away repeatedly by identifying Woyzeck in his imagination with the lizard, the cat or the donkey which are just the tools of his research (pp.417, 425, 426).

Yet Büchner is not solely concerned to present Woyzeck here as the victim of a ruthless, scientific curiosity. He shows that the Doctor's quest to extend the frontiers of medical knowledge is bound up with an irrational will to control and to possess his patient which is at odds with his belief in his dispassionate commitment to the cause of science.

This is apparent in his contemptuous condemnation of Woyzeck right at the beginning of Scene 8 *Beim Doctor*. As the Captain proclaims the awareness of his own impeccable propriety as a means of denigrating Woyzeck, so the Doctor now seeks to belittle him in the name of a lofty humanist idealism. Sweeping aside the soldier's insistence that he couldn't resist the urge to urinate in the street the Doctor condescingly declares:

> Die Natur kommt, die Natur kommt! Die Natur! Hab' ich nicht
> nachgewiesen, daß der musculus constrictor vesicae dem Willen
> unterworfen ist? Die Natur! Woyzeck, der Mensch ist frei, in dem
> Menschen verklärt sich die Individualität zur Freiheit. Den Harn nicht
> halten können! (p.417)

Büchner is obviously out to expose the class-centred, aggressive nature of the Doctor's 'idealism'. The Doctor is attempting to measure Woyzeck against a conception of freedom relevant only to those who enjoy the ordered, influential existence of the well-to-do middle-class. The dramatist makes this quite clear in a sharply satirical way by showing that the idealism which inspires the Doctor is indeed middle-class in the most narrow and banal way possible. When the Doctor congratulates himself on having achieved the freedom which is at the heart of his idealistic view of life, it becomes obvious that he (like the Captain) is not only using it as a means of diminishing his lowly patient but also that he is unaware of its conventional banality. He prides himself, for instance, on having controlled the movement of his pulse, sublimated his sneezing into a process of controlled scientific study and quelled his instinctive anger at Woyzeck's feckless behaviour. This freedom which, he believes, raises him far above the abject Woyzeck boils down in fact to the pursuit of the arch middle-class virtues of dogged self-restraint and perseverance, virtues which (as the dramatist seems ironically to imply) help preserve the supremacy of the bourgoisie at the expense of other social groups.

This sardonic deflation of the posturing grandiloquence of the Doctor's idealism is not, however, the main purpose of Büchner's polemic concern. This purpose only becomes fully apparent at the end of the scene. Here the Doctor perceives after some exchanges with Woyzeck that the latter is suffering from severe hallucinations. He greets this discovery with jubilation:

> Woyzeck Er hat die schönste aberratio mentalis partialis, die zweite Species,
> sehr schön ausgeprägt. Woyzeck Er kriegt Zulage (p.418).

The Doctor's elation here stems from the realisation that it is he who has brought about Woyzeck's dementia. By his rigid control of Woyzeck's diet he has not only manipulated his bodily functions but has succeeded also in distorting the working of his mind - reducing his patient, in fact, to a state of psychotic derangement. He, and he alone, the Doctor sees with wonder, has achieved this: he has driven this man to the very edge of insanity.

The freedom which the Doctor proclaims as the supreme capacity of
the human person is exposed here as the freedom to subject and finally
dehumanise another in the pursuit of obsessive self-aggrandisement.
For despite the Doctor's efforts to justify his experiments on Woyzeck
by claiming that they serve to extend the sum of medical knowledge,
Büchner shows that this is itself just a means to a still greater overriding
end - that of gaining 'immortality' for himself as the man who
completely changed the face of modern science (p.417).

In this probing investigation of Woyzeck's relations with his social
superiors Büchner is intent mainly on exploring the wider consequences
of his poverty. In his extreme destitution Woyzeck (the dramatist makes
clear) is not just a man without money but also a being utterly exposed,
without any effective means of defence or self-assertion in his everyday
existence. He appears in these scenes as an individual bereft of rights.
Büchner also seems to be suggesting that Woyzeck's predicament is
insoluble. The more intensely he suffers at the hands of those who have
power over him, the more deeply he is beset by an open conspicuous
anxiety which, it seems, serves only to provoke further the sadistic
energies of those who torment him.

Büchner makes it clear that Woyzeck himself is unable to understand
the nature of this fundamental and unrelenting victimisation. He is
certainly aware of his dreadful poverty and the ways in which it
restricts and demeans his existence. He also recognises that for the poor
life is unending toil and fear. The uneasy sleep of his child becomes for
Woyzeck the symbol of the poor man's whole existence:

> Was der Bub schläft. Greif' ihm unter's Ärmchen der Stuhl drückt ihn. Die
> hellen Tropfen steh'n ihm auf der Stirn; Alles Arbeit unter der Sonn, sogar
> Schweiß im Schlaf. Wir arme Leut! (p.413)

Büchner shows, however, that Woyzeck cannot begin to grasp the
extent to which the years of incessant struggle for survival in a world
which seems increasingly hostile, have eroded his emotional stability
and laid him open to a chronic, disabling sense of insecurity. The
helplessness of Woyzeck, as Büchner apprehends it, certainly lies in his
grinding poverty and the exposure it brings; but it is also inherent in his
inability to understand the long-term consequences of his destitution and
the nature of the antagonism he encounters in his life in society.

These expository scenes are informed by a cutting social anger which
is palpable throughout, although Büchner never expresses it directly in
overtly propagandist terms. These scenes show the dramatist's concern

to show the tragic development as rooted in, and impelled by the momentum of economic-social processes which none of the dramatic figures can recognise or confront. When we attempt to engage these scenes imaginatively we can only marvel at the intense visionary power with which in so short a span Büchner is able to realise such a wide and searching view of the social conditions controlling the lives of the dramatic agents. The dramatist succedes in locating the tragic development in the tense, divided provincial society which German readers in the first half of the 19th century would, I think, have recognised as their own. He has also in my view succeded in bringing to life characters who are unmistakably the creatures of this social world. Any attempt on the part of critics to dismiss or play down this particularising, empirical impetus in the conception of *Woyzeck* involves a serious weakening of the dissonant, probing character of the play Büchner actually wrote.

(3) The Social Disaffection of Marie

The revelation of the extreme vulnerability of Woyzeck in society, his poverty and impotence before those who have authority over his existence, forms a gradual process of exposition which extends throughout almost the entire dramatic action and which, as I have suggested, pervades and clarifies the presentation of the unfolding action of the tragedy. The exploration of Woyzeck's social oppression goes hand in hand with the disclosure of Marie's betrayal, with the destruction of the one relationship which holds together his whole emotional existence. The scenes early in the play (Sc.2 *Die Stadt*; Sc.6 *Kammer*) which show the eruption of Marie's passion for the Drum Major articulate a decisive and irrevocable development in the tragic action. They also form, however, an integral part of the expository process. In these scenes the dramatist explores from a different point of view the economic predicament of Woyzeck and shows the supreme cost, physical and emotional, of his desperate fight for survival. At the same time Büchner is also intent on sounding the effects of chronic poverty on the consciousness of Marie.

The playwright shows that Marie's attraction to the Drum Major for all its harsh sensual urgency, does not spring solely from sexual need. Büchner makes it increasingly clear that it is also fired by a deepening frustration in Marie, a dissatisfaction with her narrow, demeaned existence and with Woyzeck who is unable to free her from it. In her encounter with the Drum Major she is forced to face the terrible recognition that Woyzeck, the man she once loved and the father of her child, can no longer fulfil her deepest, insatiable yearning. Only now, it seems, is she able to realise the extent to which he has become a stranger, a man increasingly driven and distraught, who lives more and more in his own alien world beyond her reach (p.410).

In these brief, intensely evocative scenes Büchner realises the figure of Marie as a vital, sensual young woman driven by a longing for emotional fulfilment which is thwarted by her unworthy stunting existence. Her immediate readiness to embrace her passion for the alluring stranger also shows her unspoken will to rebel against her miserable lot.

The dramatist, then, exposes an underlying ambiguity in Marie's fateful attraction to the Drum Major which she herself is unable to recognise at first. Her conversation with her neighbour Margret in Scene 2 (pp.409f.) suggests that her response to his presence is involuntary and intensely sexual in character, that she feels challenged by the naked animal energy which charges his every movement. Her first sight of him releases a simple, awestruck reaction which reveals much more than she knows:

> Er steht auf seinen Füßen wie ein Löw (p.409).

Margret senses at once that this most fleeting and quite casual encounter has somehow displaced the inhibiting bonds of shame and restraint which normally govern her behaviour. Marie, however, far from being abashed by the sardonic sharpness of this observation, is clearly proud of her ability to feel the impact of the stranger's sexual magnetism and the sharp provocation it exudes.

Büchner stresses the spontanetiy of Marie's reactions here. He suggests that she is possessed by forces of instinct and longing which lie beyond the range of her conscious awareness and control. This is all quite clear. But, as I have already suggested, Büchner also shows other incongruous pressures at work in her emotional experience at this crucial moment in her life. Even before the Drum Major appears - Büchner suggests - Marie is a woman frustrated and deeply resentful of the deprivation which confines and depletes her existence. The dramatist explores this area of her awareness more fully in Scene 6 *Kammer* (pp.415f.). Here he shows that her seemingly headlong surrender to her infatuation is bound up with a need to prove to herself and to the world that she is worth more than her mean, constricted life:

that she deserves a much richer and more fulfilling existence than that which circumstances have forced upon her. By showing her power to attract the Drum Major she sees herself as striking back at the sheer injustice of things in the only way she can - through her beauty as a woman.

The Drum Major, confident, practised seducer that he is, senses from the first this strong impulse of revolt in Marie's responses to him and is able to exploit it for his own ends. He shrewdly presents himself to Marie not just as a man of huge sexual prowess but as someone who is socially sophisticated and successful. He is keen to impress on her that he moves with nonchalant ease through all strata of society:

> Wenn ich am Sonntag erst den großen Federbusch hab' und die weiße Handschuh, Donnerwetter, Marie, der Prinz sagt immer: Mensch, Er ist ein Kerl (p.416).

This is clearly part of a calculated strategy of seduction. Just as cunning, however, is his gift of a pair of earrings to Marie so early in their relationship, a gift which confirms his status as a man of some means, carelessly generous and boldly indifferent to the consequences of his actions (p.413). In all of this he is deliberately asserting his superiority, setting himself up in direct contrast to the poor, harried soldier who lays claims to the girl he is determined to possess.

Büchner lays bare the strong force of anger and social disaffection in Marie's tempestuous infatuation. In her encounter with the Drum Major she becomes aware for the first time of a social dissent which she has never been able to articulate fully. As she tries on her earrings she protests against a disregarding world which denies her what is hers by right:

> Unseins hat nur ein Eckchen in der Welt und ein Stückchen Spiegel und doch hab' ich einen so roten Mund als die großen Madamen mit ihren Spiegeln von oben bis unten und ihre schönen Herrn, die ihnen die Händ küssen, ich bin nur ein arm Weibsbild (p.413).

Büchner is thus out to reveal a strong impulse of social rebellion in Marie's irresistible attraction to the Drum Major. His allusive, questioning mode of presentation makes it impossible for us to assess just how it impinges on her sexual feelings or what impact it has upon them. Nonetheless the dramatist forces us to see that the intensity of her passionate surrender is bound up with, and in some degree influenced by, her urge to protest against a way of life that diminishes her and thwarts her inner potentialities.

For the sake of clarity I have tried to separate these two aspects or strands of exposition which are inseparably bound up in Büchner's conception and unified in their direct imaginative impact. Both in the scenes which enact the erupting passion of Marie and in those exploring the subjection of Woyzeck in society the dramatist is concerned to establish the poverty and social impotence of the two main figures as one of the decisive presuppositions of the tragic action. Büchner shows that even before Marie's encounter with the Drum Major Marie is in a state of latent revolt against the penury and disregard which shape her existence. He also makes it clear that even before the beginning of the action Woyzeck is trapped in a vicious cycle of dependence from which there seems no escape. The more frenziedly he has to struggle to sustain his relationship with the girl he loves, the more he appears to her as an alien demented stranger, and the less he resembles the man she once desired. At the same time it is quite clear that as he is undermined relentlessly in body and in spirit by his fight for economic survival, his need for Marie must become increasingly desperate and obsessive.

Woyzeck's love for Marie in all its deep singleminded intensity thus threatens from the first to overwhelm him. Only the readiness to compromise, to surrender his relationship with Marie as it now exists, it would seem, could resolve this apparently lethal predicament. But this is for Woyzeck something inconceivable.

II DEVELOPMENT

(1) Marie's Experience of Passion

Kammer, Scene 4 (pp.413f.) in which Woyzeck intrudes on Marie trying on the earrings given her by the Drum Major, is, as we have noted, a scene of axial dramatic importance. It fulfils a vital expository function while at the same time articulating a decisive phase in the tragic action. Here, Büchner makes clear, Marie's estrangement from Woyzeck develops into an open rift - a rift which leads directly to irrevocable catastrophe.

I have suggested that the Drum Major's gift has the effect of precipitating a latent rebellious anger in Marie and that this in turn serves to accelerate the momentum of her passion. It is noticeable here that even the unexpected intrusion of Woyzeck who makes no secret of his suspicions about the source of the earrings, fails to halt the force of her commitment to the stranger. Although she is guiltily aware of the faithfulness and generosity of Woyzeck, she knows instinctively she cannot turn back.

> Ich bin doch ein schlecht Mensch. Ich könnt' mich erstechen - Ach! Was Welt? Geht doch Alles zum Teufel, Mann und Weib! (p.413).

For Woyzeck, however, this encounter marks an experience of rupture even more terrible, so shattering in fact that he seems forced to suppress it from his conscious awareness. The dramatist succedes in revealing this by subtly suggestive means. He shows that although Marie's evasively defiant responses to Woyzeck's questions do nothing to still his suspicions about the origins of the earrings he is able to continue with his routine concerns without showing any signs of inner turmoil. He abruptly drops his uncompleted interrogation, turns his attention to their sleeping child, and giving Marie the money he has brought for her, arranges to return later in the evening (p.413). Yet in these few fateful moments, it seems, a horrifying realisation has invaded his mind. It seems that the very sight of Marie posing before the mirror with the unfamiliar earrings has triggered a subconscious process of perception which he cannot confront. To suppress the lurking recognition of her unfaithfulness he is driven, it appears, to seize hold of his everyday preoccupations in a despairing attempt to maintain his grip on a known, stable world. The futility of his struggle to escape the excruciating certainty which lies in the recesses of his mind becomes fully apparent on the next occasion he appears (Sc.7 *Auf der Gasse*, p.416). Here he intercepts Marie in order openly to accuse her of betraying him. We will have to look more closely at this development below (pp.45f.).

The break-down in the relationship between the two main figures shapes the form of the tragic action from this point on. It now develops largely in two separate strands: both protagonists are driven forward relentlessly on their appointed paths, each compelled by the force of an obsession which sets him implacably against the other. After Scene 4 Marie and Woyzeck meet only once (in the short bitter scene of Woyzeck's condemnation I have just mentioned, p.416), and here their opposition to one another appears total and irreconcilable.

Büchner does not present the devleopment of Marie's passion as a coherent emotional process. He evokes it rather as a series of eruptive crises each pointing unrelentingly forward to the next - Marie's first sight of the majestic stranger (Sc.2), her conscious recognition of her

infatuation (Sc.4), her meeting with him in her own room (Sc.6). It is
striking that here she no longer simply acknowledges her love but
openly exults in it. She now appears as a woman aflame with love who
rejoices in her power to experience such intense sexual desire and to
release it in the man she loves. As she stands face to face with the Drum
Major in the rooom she has shared with Woyzeck she expresses a
longing instinct with wonder and pride:

> Geh' einmal vor dich hin. - Über die Brust wie ein Rind und ein Bart wit
> ein Löw - So ist keiner - Ich bin stolz vor allen Weibern (p.415).

Such simple rapture does not last long, however, When the Drum
Major, narcisstically basking in her admiration, begins to describe the
superb figure he cuts on parade, Marie scornfully derides his posturing
vanity. His subsequent attempts to embrace her drive her to a sharp
ejaculation of anger. But this, as it turns out, only conspires to intensify
the force of the seducer's will to which Marie finally succumbs in
helpless resignation:

> Meinetwegen. Es ist alles eins! (416).

Büchner subtly counterposes this scene with the earlier one, also
entitled *Kammer* (Sc.4), in which Marie still struggled to acknowledge
the compelling power of her passion. Her eager, open embracing of her
love is now manifest not only in the fact that she has welcomed the
Drum Major into her room but also in the explicit and provocative
manner of her speech. Büchner's aim, however, is not merely to
emphasize these contrasts and the emotional shift they reveal. He is just
as concerned to expose the persisting tension in Marie's feelings, her
susceptibility to constraints in her own self which he has not been able
to overcome. Here, as in her earlier self-confrontation, she fights in
vain to come to terms with emotions which seem to change violently and
without warning. Even at this point when she seems to have made her
crucial decision and stands face to face with the man who inflames her
desire, Marie is still beset by doubts which collide directly with her
underlying awareness of the inevitability of her passion.
    In these scenes the dramatist is intent on exposing the tensions in
Marie's experience of passion. At times she openly exults in its
fulfilling power and the sense of release it brings her. At others,
however, she seems strangely detached from her obsessing love and
regards it as an alien force which disrupts her awareness of her own

selfhood. At such moments her passion confronts her not as a force of liberation but as a threat to her being, her deepest inner potentialities. Büchner thus presents Marie in her remorseless attraction to the Drum Major as a woman divided. Her hunger for self-realisation is constantly bound up with deep feelings of remorse and self-estrangement. The dramatist shows in these scenes that Marie despite all her eager commitment to her passion is not able to overcome this contradiction in herself. When her sexual desire is at its most intense she is certainly able for a time to suppress her latent sense of guilt; but, as Büchner forces us to see, her infatuation is never able to gather up and fuse all her disparate energies and aspirations in a supreme unifying experience of inner renewal. Even when her passionate sensuality seems at its most triumphant Marie thus appears as vulnerable and threatened, a vibrant but essentially inexperienced young woman driven by overwhelming archaic forces in herself she cannot understand or control.

(2) The Sexual Jealousy of Woyzeck

The dramatist presents the other main strand in the tragic development - the eruption of sexual anger in Woyzeck - as an equally hidden and consuming process. Here too Büchner's spasmodic, discontinuous mode of presentation reflects in direct scenic terms the dark, disruptive nature of the upheaval which convulses the protagonist. In this he is openly breaking with the traditional formal categories of classical drama. He does not establish a clear coherent link between the dawning of Woyzeck's first suspicions of Marie's unfaithfulness and its development into a devouring certainty that drives him to kill the girl he loves: Büchner presents this as the central shaping dynamic of the tragic action but he presents it as an unsearchable inner movement which resists diagnostic psychological elucidation. He grasps the hero's destructive rage as an impenetrable, irrational force, born in the depths of his being which Woyzeck himself is unable to engage as a conscious willing agent.

In the unfolding of this part of the dramatic development Scene 4 *Kammer* (pp.413f.) assumes a crucial determining importance. For although Woyzeck here recoils (as we have seen) from the conscious achknowledgement of Marie's betrayal, a shattering recognition is already taking possession of his mind. When he next appears (Sc.7 *Auf der Gasse*, p.416) he seems like a man whose world is in ruins and who is gripped by a pervading sense of futility. It is apparent straight away that he confronts Marie here in a public place not in order to gain proof

of her unfaithfulness (which would imply some residual doubt), but
simply to assert the horror of her guilt. Such an infinite betrayal, he
declares, should have left some terrible mark of disfigurement upon
her:

> Hm! Ich seh nichts. O, man müßt's sehen, man müßt's greifen könne mit
> Fäusten (p.416)

This certainty of Marie's guilt brings with it a sense of violation
which goes beyond his merely personal existence and threatens the
ultimate cosmic order:

> Eine Sünde so dick und so breit. Es stinkt, daß man die Engelchen zum
> Himmel hinaus rauche könnt (p.416)

Woyzeck speaks here as a man utterly dispossessed, torn by the
awareness of a loss beyond all understanding. Nothing Marie can do or
say is able to touch this devastating certainty that she has betrayed him
and thus defiled a trust which is ultimately sacred.

Editors of Woyzeck have disagreed about the way in which Büchner
would finally have presented this phase of the dramatic action had he
been able to revise the play. Lehmann has clearly assumed that the
dramatist's impelling aim was to internalise the tragic process and he
has set the scenes in a sequence which powerfully reflects the
compulsive inner force of the hero's rage. Some recent editors,
however, have questioned Lehmann's interpretation of the dramatist's
intentions here. Poschmann and Guthrie, for instance, have claimed,
that this scene *Auf der Gasse* (Sc.7 in Lehmann's version) should follow
Straße (Sc.9 pp.418f. in Lehmann's edition) in which the Captain with
sly, disingenuous cruelty tells Woyzeck of Marie's infidelity. The logic
of this argument is clear. If the Captain's revelation precedes Woyzeck's
denunciation of Marie we have a firm line of external development
which is both probable and immediately comprehensible. Lehmann
must of course have been aware of these considerations. However, he
has taken the bold decision to subordinate the claims of verisimilitude
and clear dramatic causality in order to enforce what he sees as the
essential inwardness of Büchner's tragic perception. One has, of course,
to acknowledge both sides of the problem here, but it seems to me that
Lehmann's solution is not just imaginative but in keeping with the
dramatist's vision of Woyzeck as a man engulfed in a nightmare
experience of betrayal and driven by dislocating forces in himself which

cut him off from the surrounding world. I personally would accept Lehmann's editorial judgment (or rather intuition) here while at the same time conceding that it has a considerable cost. In his version of the play the scene *Straße* is deprived of decisive precipitating force and fulfils a merely confirmatory, clarifying function - a function which seems quite incongruous with its powerful, intrinsically dramatic character.

It is unlikely that editors of *Woyzeck* will ever be able to solve this problem in a way which is wholly satisfactory. In fact, it seems to me that the contradictory textual indications here may be symptomatic of a deeplying tension in the attitude of the dramatist himself. Büchner was possibly groping towards some kind of accommodation between the demands of a scenically strong and intelligible plot-structure and the pressures of his quest for a experimental dramatic mode in which outward action was largely subsumed into the momentum of the hero's subjective experience. He may have been struggling, in other words, to find ways of making traditional categories of dramatic form responsive to his evolving conception of a radical new psychological tragedy. This must in the end, of course, remain essentially a matter of speculation.

But however we try to interpret Büchner's intentions here, there can be no doubting his concern to internalise the tragic action in the scenes which follow. In the scene which comes immediately after *Straße* (Sc.9) he shows Woyzeck as a man so wholly possessed by the certainty of Marie's unfaithfulness that the process of her seduction is present to his senses with overwhelming, hallucinatory clarity. In this scene *Die Wachtstube* (Sc.10, pp.420f.) Woyzeck is trapped at his post on sentry-duty yet he is able to see and feel Marie in the grip of the Drum Major at a dance taking place in the town. So powerful is this vision of her sensual excitement and desire that the world seems to spin and he finds it hard to breathe:

> Ich muß hinaus. Es dreht sich mir vor den Augen. Was sie heiße Händ habe. Verdammt Andres! (p..421)

In the grip of this disabling apprehension Woyzeck is drawn helplessly to the inn where Marie is dancing so that he can re-live what he has already perceived in his tortured imagination (Sc.11, pp.421f.). Here he does indeed find Marie as he had seen her in his mind's eye intoxicated by the sensual frenzy of the dance and utterly in thrall to the masterful, possessing Drum Major. Although this spectacle only confirms what he already knows his physical nearness to Marie, his ability to feel her almost within reach, releases in him a new savage access of despair. Once again he is ravaged by a sense of the absoluteness of Marie's treachery and is driven to see it as an act of apocalyptic horror:

> Warum bläßt Gott nicht die Sonn aus, daß Alles in Unzucht sich ubernanderwälzt, Mann und Weib, Mensch und Vieh (p.422).

Even after he has withdrawn to a lonely place away from the inn the sounds of Marie's insatiable desire and the beat of the conniving music still pound in his ears (Sc.12, *Freies Feld*, p.422). Here the awareness of a wider conflict again overwhelms him but now in a quite new and paralysing way. From out of the earth, on the movement of the wind he hears the transfixing voices commanding him to exact vengeance: to carry out the act he has refused to contemplate, to kill the girl who has betrayed him:

> Immer zu! immer zu! Still Musik. *Reckt sich gegen den Boden.* Ha was, was sagt ihr? Lauter, lauter, - stich, stich die Zickwolfin todt? stich, stich die Zickwolfin todt. Soll ich? Muß ich? Hör ich's da auch, sagt's der Wind auch? Hör ich's immer, immer zu, stich todt, todt (p.422).

The immense power of *Woyzeck* as a tragic drama stems in large part from the ability of the playwright to evoke the force of the hidden, implacable compulsion which governs the mind of the hero. Büchner suggests that the latent will to kill Marie is already inherent in Woyzeck's recognition of her betrayal, but that he refuses desperately to acknowlege it. The insistent command of the voices marks the erupting into consciousness of a compulsion which has already consumed his subliminal self. However, despite Woyzeck's helpless submission to the power of the voices he still recoils in some part of his being from the unthinkable horror of the task they impose upon him. The anguished, incredulous question 'Soll ich? muß ich?' (p.422) shows his deep emotional revulsion from the inexorable dictates of his subconscious will.

His attempt to evade the appalling power of the voices soon proves, however, to be futile. It drives him into a brief, pointless confrontation with the Drum Major which, as Büchner makes very clear, merely forces him to recognise fully the force of the necessity which engulfs him (Sc.14, *Wirtshaus* p.423).

The most striking aspect of this short, bitter encounter is that Woyzeck fails to challenge the Drum Major as the man who has robbed him of Marie. Although he is prepared to provoke the drunken, strutting seducer, he shrinks in the end from openly asserting his right to the girl he loves. This failure is revealing. The dramatist seems to be suggesting that in some inarticulate depth of his mind Woyzeck realises that all his pent-up, jealous fury at the Drum Major has no final relevance to the unfaithfulness of Marie: that this ultimate act of treachery concerns him and her alone and that even victory over her seducer could not change this. This recognition entails, however, the acceptance of his bondage to the voices.

The dramatist is concerned to evoke this sense of ultimate submission at the end of the scene. The disabling fatalism which prostrates Woyzeck here does not flow simply (Büchner suggests) from his surrender to the superior physical strength of the Drum Major. It arises rather out of a more profound, elemental consciousness of impotence, an acceptance of his final helplessness before the ravaging forces of destruction in his own self.

Büchner seems intent on emphasizing the totality of Woyzeck's surrender to the voices by contrasting his resignation after his struggle with the Drum Major with his energetic preparations for the murder in the very next scene (Sc.15, *Kramladen*, p.424). The dramatist shows here that Woyzeck is so consumed by his murderous purpose that he is oblivious to all other considerations, even that of his own safety. In considering the purchase first of a pistol then of a knife he is blind to the fact that he is laying up severely incriminating evidence which could prove his undoing. In this apparent indifference to his own safety we can sense, I think, the maiming force of a pervasive despair. It is as if Woyzeck recognised intuitively that his life after Marie's death was a matter of little importance to him. Even as he prepares to kill Marie he seems to acknowledge that life without her could have no meaning.

It is thus no surprise that when Woyzeck appears in the next scene (Sc.17, *Kaserne* p.425), he is making arrangements for his own death. As he gives the bewildered Andres instructions about the disposal of his pathetically few, meagre belongings, he recites the seemingly equally insignificant facts of his life as a soldier, as these are laid down in his military papers. Woyzeck does not explain to his friend why he is acting in this strangely solemn, formal way. It is clear to the spectator, however, that as Woyzeck prepares for the killing of Marie he also makes preparations for his own death. There is no indication whether he is here envisaging the possibility of his trial and execution as a murderer or whether he may be contemplating suicide. Either way it seems once again that Woyzeck is unable to envisage a life after Marie is

dead. But all we can deduce from his final enigmatic words is that he
senses the imminence of death, is conscious of its inescapable yet
unpredictable power:

> Ja Andres, wann der Schreiner die Hobelspän sammelt, es weiß niemand,
> wer sein Kopf drauf lege wird (p.425).

III CATASTROPHE

(1) The murder of Marie

This represents Woyzeck's final preparation for his supreme act of
retribution. When he next appears on stage it is to take Marie to the
lonely place where he will kill her (Sc.17 *Kaserne* p.425). As he
approaches her his manner is seemingly quite dispassionate but impelled
by a quiet, ominous authority. His summons to her is curt and
powerful, and seems in fact to signify that she must know the nature of
his mission and accept it. And Marie is indeed immediately gripped by
a deep foreboding of disaster. At the moment of Woyzeck's appearance
she is still haunted, it seems, by the desolating pessimism of the
Grandmother's Märchen and it is as if some hypnotic force were
undermining her will and driving her helplessly to follow him to the
place of her destruction.

In her desperate attempt to hold at bay her deepening terror Marie
struggles to cling to the ordinary, trusted circumstances of her existence
in the hope, it seems, of warding off Woyzeck's uncanny power over
her (Sc.20, *Marie und Woyzeck*, pp.427f.). She complains that she
cannot continue because of the dark, the cold, the need to prepare the
evening meal - in each case clearly seeking a pretext to return to the
security of a world where she is not alone and so utterly vulnerable.
Büchner seems to stress the pettiness of all these objections of Marie's in
order to point up the momentous implacable force of Woyzeck's
murderous determination. Nonetheless when he has to carry out the
appalling deed itself he has to work himself up into a frenzy of
destructive rage in order to carry it through to its end:

> Nimm das, und das! Kannst du nicht sterbe? So! so! Ha sie zuckt noch,
> noch nicht, noch nicht? Immer noch? *Stößt noch einmal zu.* Bist du tot?
> Tot! Tot! (p.428).

The murder of Marie forms a horrifying dramatic climax but not the tragic conclusion of Büchner's play. Although Woyzeck seems driven by a deadening despair in the scenes leading up to the murder and appears, as we have noted, on several occasions resigned to his own death, he is not tempted by the thought of suicide. On the contrary, once he has killed Marie all his actions are impelled by a compelling wordless instinct of survival. His energies now seem wholly directed at avoiding detection at all costs.

This is strikingly apparent in his return to the inn, the scene of his most excruciating pain and humiliation, immediately after the murder (Sc.22, *Das Wirtshaus*, p.428f.). Although he may not recognise it consciously, he seems moved to come back here by a need for company, by an atavistic sense that the closeness to his fellow men will make him safe. He may even have gone further and considered that the people in the inn would be able to provide him with an alibi which could establish his innocence. But whatever the motives for his return to the inn the visit does not work out as he had expected. Far from making him feel more secure it has the effect of increasing alarmingly his consciousness of exposure. The sight of his blood-soaked arm makes him the object of widening curiosity and precipitates the quite false assumption that he is under suspicion, that his guilt is written for all to see in the stains of Marie's blood. Woyzeck's blustering, aggressive reactions to the surrounding onlookers reveals the mounting panic within him:

> Teufel, was wollt ihr? Was geht's euch an? Platz! oder der erste - Teufel! Meint ihr ich hätt jemand umgebracht? Bin ich Mörder? (p.429).

This belief that he is under suspicion triggers the horrified realisation in Woyzeck that he has dropped the murder weapon when he was disturbed just after killing Marie (Sc.23, *Abend* p.430). He returns in panic to the scene of the murder and tries to dispose of it safely by throwing it as far as he can out into a pond (Sc.24, *Woyzeck an einem Teich*, p.430).

Even this does not ease his profound anxiety, however. Now that it is too late he is tortured by the thought that he may not have thrown it far enough. He asks himself whether it might be found before it rusts or whether he should have broken it before trying to hide it in the pond. Still troubled he turns his attention to the most immediately pressing task of cleaning the blood-stains, the direct and irrefutable evidence of his crime, from his clothes and body.

Throughout these scenes the dramatist emphasizes the consuming intensity of Woyzeck's fear of discovery. It possesses him with such force that it seems to drive out of his waking mind the thought of his terrible crime itself. This seems at first sight very surprising since it contradicts the repeated suggestion in earlier scenes that Woyzeck could not conceive of a life after Marie's death. If we compare his reactions here with his behaviour before the murder we can sense, I think, that Büchner is presenting Woyzeck's frenetic anxiety not just as a quite natural fear of arrest and punishment but as a subliminal protective mechanism - an attempt to repress from his conscious awareness the memory of the unthinkable atrocity he has committed and of the spiritual devastation it must wreak upon him. Büchner, as we shall see, appears to confirm this impression in the final scene of the play.

(2) The tragic Endings

Woyzeck as we know it comes to an end with two scenes each of which provides its own separate, deeply disturbing climax. The first of these (Sc.26, p.431) shows an autopsy being conducted on a corpse which, we must assume, is that of Marie. This abrupt, disconcerting scene is made up of only one short speech - a speech, however, which is immensely expressive in its far-reaching reverberative pessimism. In this the bailiff expresses his great satisfaction at the clear-cut, dramatic violence of the murder which has taken place and at the professionally challenging state of the body before him.

Here at the end of the action Büchner is re-asserting from a new and disturbing point of view the angry condemnation of contemporary society which, as we have seen, informed his presentation of earlier parts of the tragic development. He is clearly out to show in the attitude of the court-official a kind of mental detachment which implies a profound indifference to human suffering and ultimately to life itself. The *Gerichtsdiener*, as the dramatist makes clear, is so enclosed in his own professional concerns, that he remains blind to the agony and terror of the beautiful young woman whose corpse lies before him.

Büchner is here taking up socially critical concerns explored earlier in the play and attempting in particular to relate the attitude of the court-functionary to the preoccupations of the Doctor. The similarity is in fact close and highly revealing. As the Doctor can only regard the racked and increasingly disordered mind of Woyzeck as an object of experimental curiosity, so the officer of the court is only able to see the body of the murder-victim as nothing more than a *corpus delicti*, a focus for his specialised forensic skills. Both these representatives of institutionalised authority carry out their professional functions, which represent their main involvement in the corporate life of society with a detachment empty of humane, moral concern. The dramatist has already gone to some lengths to show that for the Doctor medical knowledge has lost its primary meaning as an instrument of human healing and renewal and has become a means of personal self-assertion and aggrandisement. Now he is intent on showing that the *Gerichtsdiener* has no interest in the demands of justice, in the achievement of humane, socially constructive legal judgments. He too, it appears, is concerned mainly with the exhibition of his narrow specialised skills, and thus with his status and professional standing. Like the Doctor, Büchner suggests, he is not just without pity but lacking in that basic openness of mind and imagination which is the precondition of all genuine moral concern. In the attitude of the court-official he exposes again that 'verachtenden Egoismus' characteristic of those who exercise institutionalised power in a divided, impersonal society.

At the end of the tragic development, at a point of supreme emotional intensity, Büchner powerfully re-asserts his socially critical preoccupations which had been driven out of the forefront of imaginative attention by the tension of the murder-scenes. In this brief and sharply disconcerting scene the dramatist is pointing up the social alienation of the two main figures and forcing us to consider once again the nature of their exposure in a world alien and seemingly inimical to their existence.

The final scene of the play, as we have it here, presents a quite different kind of conclusion which although apparently narrower in scope is equally powerful in its sense of tragic finality (Sc.27, *Der Idiot. Das Kind. Woyzeck,* p.431). Here the haunted murderer shaken by his experience of antagonism in the inn and by a deepening fear of self-betrayal, returns home to see his son again. The depth of Woyzeck's longing is immediately apparent in the way he makes straight for the child, conspicuously ignoring the simple-minded youth who is looking after it. The child, however, recoils from his embrace and in obvious distress begins to scream. The emotional impact of this rebuffal on Woyzeck is immense. The force of his dismay is such that he loses the power of articulate speech and can only exclaim, 'Herrgott', two short syllables pregnant with intense, disbelieving grief.

Woyzeck seems here to undergo an experience of fundamental loss. It is as if this rejection by his own child releases in him an awareness of a desolation from which there is no escape. We can sense a link, it seems to me, between the alienation of the hero after the death of Marie and his rejection by his own child and that of the orphan in the Grandmother's tale who has seen the void at the heart of the universe and is condemned to an unending, hopeless loneliness (p.427). Perhaps Woyzeck senses here that he too is alone and now has nothing left to live for.

It may well be, as some critics like Benn have claimed, that Büchner intended, had he lived longer, to extend the action of the play to include the trial and execution of Woyzeck.[4] This would certainly have brought his drama closer to the story of the historical Woyzeck and lent it a more highly developed documentary character. In my view however, the play as it stands does create a powerful sense of tragic completeness. It is, of course, not clear whether Woyzeck will be apprehended and convicted of murder or whether he might yet escape the forces of the law. Nonetheless, in a deeper sense the ending is not open or inconclusive. The last two scenes come together with an imaginative force which brings the action, it seems to me, to an intense emotional finale.

The provocative re-statement of the social victimisation of the protagonists in the penultimate scene leads on to the revelation of the spiritual estrangement of Woyzeck and in so doing gathers up the shaping impulses of Büchner's conception in a way which lends the action of the play a strong moral, if not dramaturgical, coherence. Anything that happens to Woyzeck from now on, we feel, can only be at worst a confirmation or fulfilment of that ultimate desolation of spirit which already possesses him.

NOTES

1. For a good general survey of this and other aspects of dramatic theory in the 19th century see Dieter Kafitz, *Grundzüge einer Geschichte des deutschen Dramas von Lessing bus zum Naturalismus* (Königstein/Ts., 1982) pp.12ff.; 132ff.

2. All editors now seem to accept this scene 'Freies Feld' as the opening scene of the play. John Guthrie gives a clear and perceptive summary of the reasons for this in *Lenz and Büchner: Studies in Dramatic Form* (Frankfurt am Main, 1984) pp.121ff. and more recently in his Blackwell edition of the play (Oxford, 1988) pp.27f.

3. See e.g. Arthur H. Knight, *Georg Büchner* (Oxford, 1951) p.118. Benn, *The Drama of Revolt*, pp.242, criticizes such genial views of the figure and gives a much more sombre and convincing interpretation of Büchner's critical aims.

4. See Benn, *The Drama of Revolt*, pp.256f.

CHAPTER FOUR

SOCIAL INSIGHT AND TRAGIC AWARENESS: THE IMAGINATIVE WORLD OF WOYZECK

I Critical Approaches to *Woyzeck*

Few works can ever have divided critical opinion as sharply and, it seems, as irreconcilably as *Woyzeck*. It would be wrong to put this down mainly to the uncertainties which still surround the form of the text and to persisting speculation about Büchner's final artistic intentions, important as these factors certainly are. The controversy which still dominates discussions of the play reflects, I think, a quite fundamental problem of interpretation. Despite all the intense critical effort scholars have expended on the study of *Woyzeck* in recent years they have not been able to come to any broad general agreement about the basic impetus of Büchner's tragic perception. It is very evident, in particular, that they still hold conflicting views on the nature of the dramatic motivation - on the forces which impel the development of the action and determine the catastrophe - and thus by implication on Büchner's vision of the world in which the play is set.

There seems to be some profound ambiguity inherent in the conception of the tragedy which critics have found very hard to define, much less to confront. After all these years we still seem no nearer an understanding of the kind of play *Woyzeck* actually is, and of what Büchner was ultimately seeking to achieve as a dramatist.

At the heart of this intractable problem of interpretation, it seems to me, is the playwright's shifting, peculiarly elusive perception of the interaction between the dramatic characters as centres of personal feeling and volition, and the constraining pressures of society which pervade their experience. Critics have argued tirelessly about the degree to which the individual figures are capable of personal action, about the extent to which their innermost and seemingly most private impulses and aspirations are shaped by the forces of their environment in ways they themselves cannot acknowledge.[1]

At one critical extreme commentators have argued, coherently and often with considerable persuasive force, that Büchner has succeded in creating a completely new and uncompromising form of deterministic social tragedy. Marxist critics in particular have tended to emphasize what they see as the great historical significance of this tragic conception. No critic has argued this view more strongly and provocatively than Hans Mayer whose disucssions of *Woyzeck* are still among the most widely quoted and fiercely debated. Büchner's revolutionary achievement as a playwright - Mayer claims - is that he has created a tragic mode which supersedes the notion of personal agency. The protagonist in *Woyzeck* is not the individual but the implacable force of social process which determines the tragic movement at every level and in its every aspect:

> Was treibt Woyzeck ins Verbrechen?, so wird hier gefragt. Die mögliche Antwort des Psychiaters: der Wahnsinn, kann nicht gelten; sie löst nur die neue und tiefere Frage aus: und was treibt diesen Menschen Woyzeck in die Verstrickung und Umnachtung des Geistes? Mit aller Schonungslosigkeit und Helligkeit aber antwortet das Drama, indem sein Held die Antwort gleichsam vorlebt: Die Armut, die 'Umstände' seines materiellen Lebens treiben jenen Woyzeck in die Umdüsterung, in die Auflösung seiner Bindung zur Umwelt, ins Verbrechen. (...) Das Verbrechen ist aus der gesellschaftlichen Lage erklärt, die determinierende Kraft dessen, 'was in uns lügt, hurt, stiehlt, und mordet', als soziale Lebenslage und Seinslage erkannt, in die der einzelne unabänderlich hineingeboren und verstrickt ist. Woyzecks Tun erscheint hier, ebenso wie das seiner Peiniger und Gegenspieler, als Wirkung und Produkt sozialer Funktionen und Seinslagen. Verschiedenheit der sozialen Lagen bestimmt die Verschiedenheit der Anschauungen über Sitte und Moral, entscheidet über Glücksmöglichkeit und Aufstiegschance. Nirgends ist das klarer vorgeführt und ergreifender gestaltet als in Woyzecks Gespräch mit dem Hauptmann.[2]

At the other end of the critical spectrum many more 'literary', and in general conservative, critics indebted in varying degree to the idealistic traditions of German drama, have tried to show that Büchner's conception is in fact grounded in the basic inherited categories of classical tragedy and represents a historically important attempt to renew and extend these categories in the middle of the 19th century. Kurt May, for example, who is certainly one of the most influential advocates of this critical tendency, makes a determined effort to defend what he regards as the essential formal autonomy of *Woyzeck*. He argues in the most forthright and challenging terms that the tragic momentum in Büchner's play is shaped not by extra-personal agencies but by the driving, in-born passions of the dramatic characters, passions of such uncontrollable force that they contrive to negate the constricting influence of environmental forces. May pours scorn on those who attempt to see the action of *Woyzeck* as the mechanical embodiment of impersonal historical-social processes:

> Wenn sich ein heißblütiges Weib einem bärenstarken Kerl an den Hals schmeißt und der schmählich verratene Ehemann darüber zum Messer greift, so mögen die Anreize und verstärkenden Antriebe dazu aus den gesellschaftlichen Lebensverhältnissen kommen. Aber das Geschehen gründet in einer primitiven Schicht von urmenschlich-elementarer Allmenschlichkeit, die zu allen Zeiten und überall jegliche gesellschaftliche Ordnung durchschlagen wird. Jene Deutung - und wäre sie auch die des Dichters selbst - ist doch nur eine gesellschaftskritische Abstraktion aus einer reicheren und komplexeren Wirklichkeit.[3]

It is very instructive to set these two radical, conflicting interpretations of *Woyzeck* side by side. Like almost all subsequent Marxist discussions of the play Hans Mayer sees the hero's murder of the girl who betrays him as the inevitable outcome of a relentless process of victimisation which has entrapped Woyzeck from the moment of his lowly birth in a divided, exploitative society. The cumulative pressures of poverty and social subjection - Mayer insists - drive the helpless soldier into a deeply disturbed, psychotic state in which it only needs the unfaithfulness of Marie to drive him into his demented outburst of self-destroying violence.

The most striking aspect of Mayer's interpretation here is his marked concern to play down the signficance of Woyzeck's love for his mistress as a determinative motivating force in the tragic economy. In his assessment the hero's experience of betrayal is just the final precipitating pressure on a mind already in process of dissolution, the last step in a life-long, grinding momentum of social oppression from which there is no escape.

The main thrust of May's analysis of the play is precisely to refute this view of Woyzeck as a passive, victimized hero. On the contrary (May argues) he is an emotionally intense, assertive being who, despite his life of poverty and social disregard, shows himself capable of a sustained, single-minded devotion to the girl he loves. This is for May the heart of the matter. In the sheer power of his love Woyzeck rises (in May's view) above the destructive pressures of his day-to-day existence and realises his inherent possibilities as a human being. For Kurt May and for the many subsequent critics who have accepted the essential premisses of his interpretation *Woyzeck* , for all its particularised setting and concrete social concerns, is in the last analysis a tragedy of near-mythic simplicity, a tragedy of inescapable timeless passion, of man's irrational, vulnerable nature.

These two irreconcilably opposed approaches have continued to govern studies of *Woyzeck* throughout the past three decades despite the fact that our general understanding of Büchner's work as a whole has advanced immeasurably in this period.[4] We have to ask ourselves how it is possible that critics have been able to put forward at one and the same time such conflicting views of a play in which the main developments of the action are apparently so clear-cut and beyond dispute. And this leads irresistibly on to the crucial practical question: how can we attempt to penetrate the seemingly intransigent ambiguity which still contrives to divide critical opinion? There are no short-cuts. Whether we like it or not, the only way forward, I am convinced, is to re-examine closely Büchner's peculiarly shifting, probing view of the confusing interplay of self and society which lies at the very heart of his tragic conception.

II The Tragic Hero and the historical Woyzeck

The powerful analytical drive of Büchner's creative imagination and the force of his socially critical preoccupation would seem enough in themselves to undermine May's view, that the tragic action in *Woyzeck* is only superficially influenced by environmental forces. However, even if we accept the shaping power of this empirical concern in the play's conception, we still have to proceed with extreme caution. For although Büchner seems, as we have noted, to emphasize the poverty and social bondage of Woyzeck throughout the action, he is intent on presenting the dependence of his hero on environmental forces in much more equivocal terms than the factual accounts of the historical Woyzeck would lead us to expect. As Büchner gets to grips with his material he becomes increasingly concerned to assert the individuality of the tragic protagonist in ways which force him to deviate significantly from the detailed records before him. The Clarus-reports and the accounts of the trial seem to estalish a coherent picture of the Leipzig soldier as an introverted, confused individual who had led a drifitng, drably dissolute existence, who had been out of work for long spells and was addicted, albeit in a listless and curiously apathetic way, to drink and gambling. Woyzeck was also at the age of forty one (Frau Woost was forty six) a man with a lengthy and chequered sexual past. He had had several affairs before that with Frau Woost, and had had an illegitimate child by an earlier mistress. In a still earlier relationship he had even threatened to kill the woman with whom he was living in a sporadic outburst of jealous rage.[5]

All of this is in marked contrast to the figure which Büchner creates. His hero is not just much younger but, more significantly, has about him a profound emotional innocence. In his late twenties he seems to have experienced the full intensity of love for the first time and to have regarded himself from the beginning as married to Marie. He sees their child (which is one of Büchner's most significant inventions) as proof of the permanence of their relationship and of their mutual commitment to it.

We can see here, I think, a consistent attempt on Büchner's part to free his hero from the atmosphere of squalid, dragging hopelessness which pervaded the life of the historical Woyzeck. Büchner's alterations to the factual records show his concern to create a tragic protagonist less obviously passive, less feckless than the man who stood trial in Leipzig in 1821. He presents his hero as a man possessed by a fierce, passionate yearning he can express only in his day-to-day practical devotion. Büchner's Woyzeck is a man who gives himself wholly to the girl he loves and makes an absolute claim upon her.

Unlike the real Woyzeck Büchner's hero is also intent on transforming his love into a consuming commitment which embraces his entire existence. When he calls Marie his wife he does not simply mean that he is faithful to her in a sexual sense but that he takes upon himself responsibility for every aspect of her well-being. Love for him involves providing for Marie and their child - housing, clothing and feeding them. Woyzeck's assumption of total responsibility is crucial, for it is this which makes him so completely, crushingly poor. Love in this all-embracing sense is quite simply beyond his means. I think we have to emphasize this because critics have tended to ignore it. Although Woyzeck has struggled with poverty all his life and as a common soldier belongs, as Poschmann insists, to one of the most deprived social groups, it is only his responsibilities as 'husband' and father which have driven him into his present state of utter and seemingly irredeemable destitution. In his determination to feed three mouths instead of one he makes himself a victim of poverty in a new and quite drastic way. Woyzeck, however, as Büchner presents him, undertakes this obligation as a matter of course, even though it makes his whole life a more and more desperate struggle to increase his inadequate income. The horrifying poverty which afflicts Woyzeck is thus not simply imposed on him by his social circumstances; it is in a crucial degree a burden he takes upon himself without question and without complaint. Though common sense may tell him (and also no doubt his bachelor colleagues) that it is impossible to sustain this financial burden, he embraces it as something self-evident and inescapable.

When we look at it in this way Woyzeck's love for Marie appears as an act of gigantic defiance. He refuses to accept that his poverty denies him the possibility of his love. Through his devotion for Marie the activating impulse of his whole life becomes a revolt against the cardinal fact of his destitution. The humble, subjected soldier (to whom the very notion of revolt would be unthinkable) appears here as a man who like the great rebels of classical tragedy, is bent on pursuing his passion wherever it leads and whatever the costs; as a man who challenges the nature of things as they are by the sheer persistence of his will.

Despite his obvious concern to show the social oppression of Woyzeck the dramatist is, then, also concerned to assert his individuality, to emphasize the sustained, sacrificial power of his love for Marie. Far from portraying him simply as a passive, broken victim of society, as some critics have claimed, Büchner presents him also as a man who seeks single-mindedly to defy the thwarting force of his circumstances.

But here again we must be careful. To put the matter in this bland way is misleading. It ignores the essentially exploratory, questioning nature of Büchner's conception of Woyzeck's experience. Even as he shows the great emotional energy and commitment of his hero, he also contrives to evoke the peculiar exposure, the drivenness at the heart of his longing for love. The very intensity of Woyzeck's devotion, the dramatist seems to suggest, betrays the insidious sense of alienation which shapes his whole affective existence. Büchner draws us repeatedly to sense the underlying force of despair in his passion for Marie, the blind search for hope and fulfilment which impel his devotion. In the course of the action Woyzeck comes himself to plumb the full depths of his need of her. At the moment of disaster, when he is driven to face the unthinkable, he seems for a moment to glimpse the horror that lurks behind his love. Now, as if in an intuitive flash of recognition he sees that Marie is, in the most fundamental sense, all he has: that his love for her is all that stands between him and utter despair (p.420)

Büchner thus presents the love of Woyzeck for Marie, in a way which constantly frustrates our search for clear logical understanding. He forces us to question the relationship between the force of the hero's passion and his deforming social existence but denies us any directing, conclusive answers. In depriving us of the possibility of understanding the nature of Woyzeck's passionate attachment, however, the dramatist also makes it impossible for us to grasp the tragic action as a whole in firm, coherent moral terms.

III Paranoia and metaphysical Despair

The dramatist also forces us to explore with equal insistence one other basic aspect of Woyzeck's tragic experience: his visionary awareness of supernatural hostility. Büchner presents his hero - like the historical Woyzeck - as a man haunted by terrifying fantasies of violence. In the very first scene of the play he shows how the mind of Woyzeck is at times utterly possessed by his hallucinations, how he actually sees vicious acts of retribution take place before him and senses hostile forces at work around him (p.409). As I have emphasized in Chapter III above, Büchner is clearly intent on presenting these delusions of Woyzeck's as powerful, revealing symptoms of a regressive psychotic disorder.

In the course of the following scenes it becomes increasingly evident that the excruciating images of supernatural violence which take over Woyzeck's mind stem largely from the apocalyptic world of biblical prophecy. He actually witnesses the fulfilment of these prophecies here and now as he goes about his daily duties. These cataclysmic visions from the Old and New Testaments invade the mundane, empirical world and transform it for Woyzeck into a realm of transfixing horror. They uproot him from the continuities of his routine existence and thrust him, naked and helpless, into a hostile vengeful cosmos. In his subjection to these terrifying hallucinations, probably more than in any other area of his experience, Woyzeck appears as violated and utterly, untouchably bereft.

Büchner presents these compulsive fantasies of Woyzeck from an analytical, diagnostic standpoint. I think almost all critics would accept this. In their different ways they would all accept that the dramatist is concerned to use the visions which overwhelm the hero as a means of sounding the deepening psychic disorder which drives him to the very edge of mental break-down.

Here again, however, the dramatist opens up different ways of seeing and evaluating what appear to be the psychotic delusions of the hero.

As Büchner enforces this clinical view, he also seeks to draw Woyzeck's visionary experience into a wider sphere of sceptical enquiry which seems in conflict with the assumptions controlling his analytical approach. Büchner attempts intuitively, it seems to me, to link Woyzeck's crazed awareness of cosmic hostility to an on-going process of metaphysical questioning which unfolds simultaneously in different areas of the dramatic development - a process aimed, it seems, at throwing into doubt all the main officially accepted, optimistic myths - religious, scientific and cultural - which governed the outlook of mid-19th century German society.

This sceptical, deflating process of enquiry is probably most strikingly apparent in two communal scenes set at the fair and the inn which seem at first sight peripheral to the dramatic development. In the first of these (Sc.3, *Buden, Lichter, Volk,* pp.41f.) the visitors to the fair are confronted by a series of bizarre performing animals. The Fair Crier attributes to these beasts prodigious intellectual abilities which, as he sardonically insists, expose man's confident belief in his undisputed supremacy over other species. He points out that the monkey and the horse, for instance, have learnt through systematic training to perform sophisticated tricks which people assume to be beyond subhuman creatures. The monkey walks upright, wears trousers, carries a sword, and has also mastered considerable social graces. It can bow with the elegance of a nobleman and kiss like a human lover. For his 'astronomic' horse the Crier makes even grander claims. This 'animal-person', he declares, can do mental arithmetic and, though deprived of the power of speech, it can answer all kinds of intricate questions. At the same time it has the physical agility and grace normally considered the prerogative of its two-legged superiors.

Behind these claims of the Crier there lies a barbed, disturbing question: if an animal can achieve such levels of sophistication through training, what is left of man's claim to pre-eminence over all other species. Is man not just after all a product of nature?

> Das hat geheißa: Mensch sei natürlich.
> Du bist geschaffe Staub, Sand,
> Dreck. Willst du mehr sein, als Staub
> Sand, Dreck (p.412)

The Fair Crier's exhibition of his animals thus serves a cynical, disillusioning purpose. He seems intent on exposing the underlying arrogant presumption of Western Christian civilisation that reason is an absolute, the divine light in man which enables man alone of all created things to shape his destiny as a moral agent. If the Crier's claim is true, that man's so-called rational capacities represent just a sublimation of animal instinct and differ therefore from this only in degree, what grounds are there (Büchner seems to ask) for man's vain, self-serving belief that he enjoys by divine dispensation a supreme status in the universal order?

Büchner questions the inherited metaphysical confidence of contemporary European man from another point of view in *Wirtshaus* (Sc.11, p.411). Here a drunken Journeyman preaches a 'sermon' from a table in the inn before the assembled drinkers. In this he satirises the blindly optimistic conviction that the whole cosmic order has been created by Providence solely for the eternal salvation of the human race. The cynical, deriding thrust of this sermon stems from the absurd circularity of its argument, an argument made to sound weighty and august by its frequent biblical allusions and ecclesiastical echoes. Like countless orthodox preachers before him the Journeyman asks the fundamental question 'Warum ist der Mensch ? Warum ist der Mensch?', only to make a dogmatically pre-ordained reply:

> Jedoch wenn ein Wandrer, der gelehnt steht an den Strom der Zeit oder aber sich die göttliche Weisheit beantwortet und sich anredet: Warum ist der Mensch? Warum ist der Mensch? - Aber warhlich ich sage euch, von was hätte der Landmann, der Weißbinder, der Schuster, der Arzt leben sollen, wenn Gott den Menschen nicht geschaffen hätte? Von was hätte der Schneider leben sollen, wenn er dem Menschen nicht die Empfindung der Scham eingepflanzt, von was der Soldat, wenn er ihn nicht mit dem Bedürfnis sich totzuschlagen ausgerüstet hätte. Darum zweifelt nicht, ja ja, es ist lieblich und fein, aber alles Irdische ist eitel, selbst das Geld geht in Verwesung über (p.422)

Büchner seems to be suggesting here that this mode of 'reasoning', ludicrously nonsensical as it is, merely re-iterates the premises of a complacent anthropocentric theology which postulates a comforting relationship between man and a benevolent Creator and then proceeds to interpret life in a perversely selective way which inescapably enforces its original assumption.

A similarly sceptical, belittling thrust also shapes Büchner's portrayal of the two representative, middle-class figures, the Captain and the Doctor. We have already noted how the dramatist uses these figures as a means of exploring the working of destructive class-attitudes in contemporary German society. In their relations with the down-trodden, struggling Woyzeck these characters appear as the incarnation of the powerful, affluent bourgeois society which dominates his existence. To him they embody a life of unassailable security and order. In his presentation of the Captain and the Doctor the playwright seeks, however, to probe behind the mask of unquestioned social authority and to lay bare the insidious pressures of a profound inward dread at the hidden core of their experience.

In his first encounter with Woyzeck (p.414f.) the Captain projects himself primarily as a man who takes an immense pride in the disciplined propriety of his existence, who has succeded in bringing his entire life, private and social, into harmony with clear acknowledged moral norms (See above pp.16ff.). At a crucial point in the scene, however, he lets his guard slip and exposes a quite different awareness of himself. Overcome by an involuntary surge of self-pity he exposes beneath all his self-righteous complacency a despairing sense of the emptiness of his existence. Here it becomes clear that, far from being a man in control, he is a depressive, yearning being haunted by a vision of his life stretching ahead of him, a bleak, void expanse of time which he must somehow contrive to fill, but which has no value or meaning. However many the months and weeks granted to him he knows they can never amount to anything or lead anywhere; they are devoid of possibility and hope. His question 'Was will Er denn mit der ungeheuren Zeit all anfangen?', although nominally addressed to Woyzeck, crystallises all the anguish of his own tormented existence.

Büchner ironically points up these sharp discrepancies in his portrayal of the Captain. He counterposes the purposeful officer which the Captain presents to the world with the melancholic who is hidden from public view, the smug pillar of the social establishment with the haunted private man racked by a sense of futility.

The same will to sardonic exposure impels Büchner's presentation of the other representative of the dominant bourgeoisie, the Doctor. Here too Büchner is concerned to reveal the gap between the Doctor's proud view of himself and his social eminence and the deeply vulnerable man within which no one can see.

It is clear that the Doctor regards himself as a scholar committed to the cause of science which he sees as the supreme agent of human progress. The dramatist shows, however, that the Doctor's belief in his selfless dedication to the benevolent, liberating goals of science is at heart a self-deceiving, escapist illusion. In all three scenes in which the Doctor appears Büchner ironically exposes the narrow driving self-interest which motivates his manic quest for scientific discovery. This is apparent in the fact that the Doctor has no interest in a controlled systematic extension of the frontiers of medical knowledge. He strives rather for some prodigious, startling finding which will overthrow at a stroke all the work of his scientific colleagues and lend him an unquestioned supremacy over them. His aim, as he himself ingenuously admits, is to 'explode' the accepted foundations of medical research and gain immortality for himself as the man who single-handedly revolutionized modern scientific thought. Behind all his declarations of humanistic idealism the Doctor is - as Büchner ironically reveals - a harried, helpless victim of a megalomania which threatens to unhinge him. The blind desperation of his search for fame belies the arrogant confidence of his social manner and reveals a compulsive unacknowledged urge to escape the awareness of the great spiritual void within him. The Doctor, so hungry for acclaim and veneration, is a man (the dramatist suggests) in flight from himself, from the paralysing awareness of his ultimate nullity in the universal scheme of things.

When we look at Büchner's presentation of the figures of the Captain and the Doctor from this point of view, we can see his persistent concern to stress the disparity between the assertive, imposing social persona and the anguished hidden self. In their professional relationships both men seem to embody a strong, socially enforced authority, yet, as the playwright makes clear, both are in reality anguished men, each in his own way ravaged by a deep sense of existential horror and apprehension. Behind the facade of their secure, purposive lives in society the Captain and the Doctor are torn by feelings of inner emptiness and of their estrangement from a world in which they can see no ultimate sustaining meaning. In the experience of both men Büchner seeks to lay bare a disabling sense of metaphysical desolation which neither can fully articulate much less confront.

In this process of ironic exposure the dramatist, I think, is concerned to suggest some deep-lying, hidden affinities between the experience of these two middle-class figures and that of Woyzeck, affinities which remain completely suppressed in their dealings in the public world of society. The dramatist draws us to search out the hidden links between the soldier's demented awareness of supernatural hostility and the intuitions of cosmic abandonment which afflict these two men who appear as rational and 'normal' in the eyes of society. Both Woyzeck, the social outcast, and the established middle-class figures are gripped by the awful, impenetrable otherness of the world, of their ultimate alienation from a universe averse to their deepest spiritual yearning for meaning and value.

At the same time, however, Büchner is also intent on emphasizing the differences of experience separating Woyzeck from these other characters. The hero is distinguished above all by the absoluteness of his exposure to the apprehensions of horror which possess him. He appears throughout as the one figure in the play who is completely open to the irruptions of archaic, irrational terror. It consumes him with a force which threatens to destroy the very fabric of his selfhood. The two middle-class figures appear by contrast as insulated against such final exposure. They are able for much of their waking lives to hold at bay their insidious awareness of absurdity. In fact, as the dramatist ironically suggests, the Captain and the Doctor, consciously or unconsciously, exploit their secure, well upholstered positions in society in order to repel their underlying despair. Their elevated social status does not, in other words, enable them to achieve self-knowledge or moral insight; it serves rather to provide the means of extensive self-deception, of escape. Woyzeck, deprived and abused in every single area of his existence appears in this perspective as the 'poor bare forked animal', the naked man with no means of retreat, no recourse to false, consoling fantasies.

Unless I am much mistaken, Büchner is making an important distinction here between the clinical, pragmatic assessment of Woyzeck's mental state and its tragic significance. From a medical standpoint his awareness of an engulfing supernatural hostility appears as paranoiac, since it is compulsive and detached from empirical reality. In imaginative terms, in the context of the unfolding tragic process, Woyzeck's visionary consciousness of abandonment seems, however, instinct with possibilities of revelation, of tragic meaning, which are at odds with its narrow medical diagnosis.

That Büchner was aware of the potential evocative significance of Woyzeck's experience in this way is quite evident, I think, in his concern to identify his tragic hero with the cosmic orphan who is the protagonist in the Grandmother's haunting *Märchen* which so powerfully enlarges the imaginative context of the tragic action:

> Es war eimal ein arm Kind und hat kein Vater und kein Mutter, war alles tot und war niemand mehr auf der Welt. Alles tot, und es ist hingangen und hat greint Tag und Nacht. Und weil auf der Erd niemand mehr war, wollt's in Himmel gehn, und der Mond guckt es so freundlich an und wie's endlich zum Mond kam, war's ein Stück faul Holz und da ist es zur Sonn gangen und wie's zur Sonn kam, war's ein verreckt Sonneblum und wie's zu den Sterne kam, warn's klei golde Mücke, die warn angesteckt wie der Neuntöter sie auf die Schlehe steckt, und wie's wieder auf die Erd wollt, war die Erd ein umgestürzter Hafen und war ganz allein und da hat sich's hingesetzt und geweint und da sitzes noch und ist ganz allein (p.427).

The intense evocative energy of this tale, narrated just before the tragic catastrophe, stems from its power to focus the wordless, uncomprehended agony of Woyzeck und lend it heightened, generalised expression. All his terror and desolation are gathered up in the unavailing quest of the orphan who traverses a decaying universe in the search for the creative source of life and who in the end succumbs to a dereliction which is endless and infinite.

In the *Märchen* Büchner is concerned, it seems, to elevate the tragic experience of Woyzeck by recasting it in an enhancing mythical form which transcends the narrowness of the play's setting and the social humility of the inarticulate hero. The cosmic anguish of the orphan magnifies the scope of Woyzeck's suffering and lends it wider, representative expression without (Büchner may be suggesting) in any way inflating its immediate, personal intensity. For Woyzeck, just like the stricken child, gives himself utterly and is broken by a world which denies him everything.

NOTES

1.   L. Büttner, *Büchners Bild vom Menschen*, (Nürnberg, 1967), pp.53ff.
2.   H. Mayer, *Georg Büchner und seine Zeit*, (Wiesbaden, 1960), pp.331f.
3.   K. May, *Form und Bedeutung. Interpretationen deutscher Dichtung des 18. und 19. Jahrhunderts*, (Stuttgart, 1957), pp.263ff.
4.   See K. Mills and B. Keith-Smith, ed., *Georg Büchner. Tradition und Innovation*, (Bristol, 1990), pp.4ff.
5.   Lindenberger, *Georg Büchner*, pp.95f.
6.   H. Poschmann, *Georg Büchner*, (Berlin//Weimar, 1983), pp.245ff.
7.   Poschmann, *Georg Büchner*, pp.265f.

CONCLUSION

It would be hard to overstate the historical significance of *Woyzeck* It is a work of revolutionary, renewing originality which was to exercise an immense influence on German drama throughout the late 19th and early 20th centuries. We can sum up Büchner's achievement by saying with deceptive simplicity that he transformed all the received conceptions of realistic drama and in so doing opened up powerful, unrecognised possibilities for the development of modern tragedy.

If we try to see *Woyzeck* in relation to the socially critical drama of the *Sturm und Drang* we can sense at once its sharply stimulating impact on Büchner. He shares with the dissident young playwrights of the 1770's the driving will to confront the dominant traditions of heroic tragedy and to create a new kind of drama which grows out of the tensions of immediate social experience. Like his predecessors he seeks to develop the drama as an analytical, searching mode capable of exploring the peculiar vulnerability of the estranged self in an increasingly alien, depersonalised world.

When we look at *Woyzeck* in this historical perspective, it is equally clear, however, that Büchner was attempting to radicalise this inherited tradition of social drama. He significantly extends the range of the genre by bringing a new and hitherto disregarded under-class into the centre of dramatic interest and by dramatising the condition of poverty for the first time. In the context of the drama of the 1830's in Germany this is all innovative and iconcoclastic but the real source of Büchner's historical achievement lies, I believe, elsewhere: in his concerted thrust to assimilate the social drama as a realistic form to a more open, imaginatively outreaching, 'poetic' mode which was both new and controversial yet which also had profound, hidden roots in traditional conceptions of the European drama.

In *Woyzeck* the dramatist seeks (as we have seen) to establish the socially victimised, driven individual as a passionate tragic figure. He asserts the deprived, inarticulate, superstituous soldier as a protagonist of intense emotional power, a being impelled to a total tragic commitment and in the end broken by an ultimate denuding despair. In realising the figure of Woyzeck Büchner is intent on laying bare those 'veins of feeling', which, as he declares in his novella *Lenz*, lie, often unseen, in the humblest life and which are commom to all human kind. In this will to penetrate to a realm of underlying, shared human experience Büchner in his own way is fired by that quest for *das*

Allgemeinmenschliche, for the timeless, universal dimensions of man's awareness which animated the tragic dramatist of German classicism. Büchner's sense of the powerful, underived energies of love and hope informs his perception of the tragic development in *Woyzeck* and lend it a representative, near-mythical quality which is incongruous with the social humility and exposure of the characters.

This imaginative drive to surpass the restrictions of the analytical form is also apparent in Büchner's concern to grasp metaphysical awareness as an organic part of the everyday experience of the dramatic figures. He brings into being a tragic world which though socially narrow and parochial, vibrates throughout with intense cosmic menace. All the *dramatis personae* seen to live on a precipice. Even those in positions of social power are torn from the seeming security of their stable worlds by a disabling ontological dread which they seek to supress but can never fully dispel.

Throughout our discussion of Büchner's play I have tried to emphasize the intensely searching, exploratory character of his tragic conception. He does not present the action in a way which enables us to gain an intellectually firm, coherent grasp of developments and thus achieve a conclusive integrated interpretation. His mode of presentation is overtly fragmented and dissonant. He seems intent on putting forward provisional interpretative possibilities which he sets in tension with one another. As we have seen, Büchner apprehends the tragic action from constantly shifting points of view and tests one perspective, one way of seeing, against another. In this way he seems concerned throughout to interrogate the dramatic process in a way which unsettles the imaginative responses of the reader or spectator and forces him repeatedly to revise his assumptions, re-think his impressions and constantly re-discover what he has experienced. We are granted, as far as I can see, no opportunity to stand outside the tragic world, of grasping it in one comprehensive, harmonious perception. Büchner's tragic vision is impelled by an intense, searching ambivalence which is both completely distinctive and of great prophetic importance for the development of German drama.

SUGGESTIONS FOR FURTHER READING

The critical literature on Büchner and on *Woyzeck* in particular has grown immeasurably in the past few years. I have attempted here to pick out some titles which are generally available and readily accessible to English-speaking students of Büchner.

G. Baumann, *Georg Büchner. Die dramatische Ausdruckswelt*, (Göttingen, 1961).

M. Benn, *The Drama of Revolt. A critical Study of Georg Büchner*, (Cambridge, 1978).

W. Buch, *Woyzeck. Fassungen und Wandlungen*, (Dortmund, 1970).

L. Bornscheuer, *Woyzeck. Erläuterungen und Dokumente*, (Stuttgart, 1972).

L. Büttner, *Büchners Bild vom Menschen*, (Nürnberg, 1967).

H. Fischer, *Georg Büchner, Untersuchungen und Marginalien*, (Bonn, 1972).

J. Guthrie, *Lenz und Büchner. Studies in Dramatic Form*, (Frankfurt am Main, 1984).

 - ed. *Woyzeck*, (Oxford, 1988).

R. Hauser, *Georg Büchner*, (New York, 1974).

W. Hinderer, *Büchner. Kommentar zum dichterischen Werk*, (München, 1977).

M. Jacobs, ed., *Dantons Tod und Woyzeck*, (Manchester, 1954)

D. James, *The 'Interesting Case of Woyzeck'* in D. James and S. Ranawake ed. *Patterns of Change*, (Frankfurt am Main, 1990) pp.103-119.

A.H. Knight, *Georg Büchner*, (London, 1974).

E. Kobel, *Georg Büchner. Das dichterische Werk*, (Berlin, 1974).

H. Krapp, *Der Dialog bei Büchner*, (München, 1958).

H. Lindenberger, *Georg Büchner*, (Carbendale, 1964).

E. McInnes, *Das deutsche Drama des 19. Jahrhunderts*, (Berlin, 1983).

 -, *'Ein ungeheures Theater'. The Drama of the Sturm und Drang*, (Frankfurt am Main, 1987).

K. May, *Form und Bedeutung*, (Stuttgart, 1957).

H. Mayer, *Georg Büchner und seine Zeit*, (Wiesbaden, 1960).

K. Mills and B. Keith-Smith, ed., *Georg Büchner. Tradition and Innovation*, (Bristol, 1990).

H. Poschmann, *Georg Büchner*, (Berlin, 1983).

D.G. Richards, *Georg Büchner 'Woyzeck'. Interpretation und Textgestaltung*, (Bonn, 1975).

 -, *Georg Büchner and the Birth of Modern Drama*, (New York, 1977).

K. Vietor, *Georg Büchner. Politik. Dichtung. Wissenschaft*, (Bern, 1949).